LIFE
directions

Jane Kise &
David Stark

BETHANY HOUSE PUBLISHERS
MINNEAPOLIS, MINNESOTA 55438

Published by Bethany House Publishers
A Ministry of Bethany Fellowship International
11400 Hampshire Avenue South
Minneapolis, Minnesota 55438
www.bethanyhouse.com

Printed in the United States of America by
Bethany Press International, Minneapolis, Minnesota 55438

ISBN 1–55661–208–7

For Sandra Hirsh,
a wellspring of wisdom and creativity
in all we've done together...
but best of all, a dear friend.
—Jane

For Janet, Dan, and Kevin,
who have lovingly lived the adventure with me,
through all of its ups and downs, twists and turns—
experiencing God's faithful guidance through it all.
—David

LifeKeys Resources

LifeKeys

LifeKeys Discovery Workbook

LifeKeys Leadership Resource

Find Your Fit: LifeKeys for Teens

Find Your Fit Discovery Workbook

LifeDirections

SoulTypes

Work It Out

For more information: www.lifekeys.com

Jane A.G. Kise is a freelance writer and management consultant. She holds an M.B.A. from the University of Minnesota and trains people around the country on how to unlock their lives for God.

David Stark is pastor of adult education at Christ Presbyterian Church in Edina, Minnesota, and a graduate of Princeton Theological Seminary. His small-group materials, *People Together,* are widely used in churches of various denominations.

Contents

Chapter 1

"If God Is My Copilot, Why Can't I Read the Instrument Panel?"

If I rise on the wings of the dawn,
if I settle on the far side of the sea,
even there your hand will guide me,
your right hand will hold me fast.

—Psalm 139:9-10

Jane remembers a crisp, clear morning in Minnesota—the kind that often follows a blizzard:

Other than the scraping of shovels on our driveway, few sounds echoed in the bitterly cold air. No cars, for the plows hadn't passed our way yet. No children, for it was still below zero. Suddenly our ears detected the faint honking of birds in flight and we gazed up at the blue skies. So high as to be almost invisible, we spotted several silvery V's of geese passing overhead as they migrated from Canada toward warmer climes. "At least they know where to go in this weather," my husband quipped as we leaned on our shovels.

People have always envied birds. They soar unencumbered, viewing earth from a perspective we long to share. They sing pleasantly, not only cheering our lives but giving us glimpses of a carefree existence. And perhaps most mysteriously, birds know their way. They know *where* to go. They know *when* to go. Geese head south before a hard freeze ruins the northern lakes for swimming. They return north only when the spring thaw is well established.

Do you wonder where you're going? Perhaps you face a major life decision and are uncertain how to proceed. Are you worried that if you miss God's will, you'll spoil your life or hurt those closest to you? It's hard to experience a joyful Christian walk if you believe you're one step from disaster. Or are you second-guessing past choices, wondering how to get back on track if you're headed the wrong way? It's hard to follow God whole-heartedly if you're looking over your shoulder. Or are you try-ing to learn more about how God guides us before you come to an unmarked crossroads? Whatever the starting point of your journey, it's easy to envy the confident migration flights of geese. Easy, that is, if you aren't sure *if* or *how* God guides humans. But God has gifted us with guidance systems to head us toward our destination.

If the migration patterns of geese are mysteriously impressive, still more remarkable are the inborn abilities of homing pigeons.

Imagine being in a strange town and wanting to get back to your loft. No problem for homing pigeons. God designed them with not just one but *four* guidance systems that allow these birds to chart with unerring accuracy the way home. On a clear day, they use the sun to get their bearings. If it's cloudy, they sense the magnetic fields of the earth, determining their position relative to the North or South Pole. They pick up the echoes of their cries bouncing off objects around them, avoid-ing collisions with trees or cliffs. Finally, when home is in view, their eyes spot the exact location of their loft, allowing for a per-fect landing.

Documented cases report pigeons returning home from six hundred miles away in just one day. Their accuracy is so trust-worthy that as recently as World War II, army intelligence used them for sending messages. The more that scientists study this phenomenon, the more amazed they are at the incredibly complex guidance system that is naturally a part of each hom-ing pigeon.

For pigeons, getting home is vital in order to reach safety

and nourishment. While we may marvel at their abilities, the truth is that as humans our goals are more complicated. Our needs go beyond safety and nourishment to security, serenity, and significance. And to a real-life sanctity of all we are and do. "Going home," for those of us who believe in God, is being able to look back with God—confidently—over how we navigated our entire life. Were we faithful servants? Were our choices within the will of God?

Most of us agonize at one time or another over choices we face, be it what career to pursue, whom to marry, how to raise our children—the list is endless. Sometimes it seems as if heaven is silent. Yet repeatedly the Bible tells us that we can find out what God wants us to do:

> The Lord will guide you always. (Isaiah 58:11)

> In all your ways acknowledge him and he will make your paths straight. (Proverbs 3:6)

> For it is God who works in you to will and to act according to his good purpose. (Philippians 2:13)

> For we are God's workmanship, created in Christ Jesus to do good works, which God prepared in advance for us to do. (Ephesians 2:10)

The promises are present in great numbers. And if God has prepared good works for us, certainly we are supposed to be able to find out what they are!

Then why do most of us struggle to find God's will for our lives? If God guides the homing pigeons, then surely we can depend on our Creator for guidance as well—after all, "How much more valuable you are than birds!" Jesus assured us. (Luke 12:24)

So how come the birds have such an easy time getting home, while we agonize at each and every turn?

What Is the Will of God?

Part of our difficulty in discerning God's will can be traced to our misconceptions about what that will entails. We wonder what the will of God is in the midst of tragic circumstances, as if God wills such events. People talk of "finding God's will for my life" as if it were a one-time event that determined your entire future. And they assume that God's will could never match their own idea of happiness in life. But that simply isn't the picture the Bible presents. "'My food,' said Jesus, 'is to do the will of him who sent me'" (John 4:34). In other words, our very sustenance depends on doing the will of God.

Jesus said our lives would be full of joy. He didn't say, however, that everything would be smooth sailing. Actually, he guaranteed otherwise: "I have told you these things, so that in me you may have peace. In this world you will have trouble. But take heart! I have overcome the world" (John 16:33).

Jesus also said, "Whoever does God's will is my brother and sister and mother" (Mark 3:35). Doing the will of God makes the difference between being part of God's family in name only or enjoying the fellowship, closeness, and shared happiness of the ideal life with God. It's how we act out our membership in the family of God.

God's will, then, is not only about doing that which brings about the kingdom of heaven on earth, but also about living in a way that brings God's fulfillment to you personally as you become more and more like Christ. They are one and the same. True fulfillment isn't found in what you possess or whether you've measured up in the eyes of the world; it's about becoming all you can be—tapping into all of the potential God has given you. Only God knows what will truly satisfy the longing inside each of us. If you decide not to seek God's will for your life, not only does the kingdom lose your contribution, you lose the chance of finding the fulfilling life you were meant to live.

One way to look at doing the will of God is in the broad sense: We can follow general principles, such as the Ten Commandments, Micah's edict "to act justly and to love mercy and to walk humbly with your God" (6:8), and the teachings of Jesus on servanthood, forgiveness, and loving your brother as yourself.

Some people say that is the only way we can track the will of God, by staying within these moral boundaries. And for a lot of areas of our lives, determining general principles is enough.

But God hasn't stopped speaking to us. The Bible is God's first and last Word, the test of all things. Yet it isn't God's only word. We can experience guidance through other God-given systems as well. God is ready to guide us more specifically so we can find when, where, and how to fulfill God's will for *our* lives; discover the purposes for which we were created; rejoice in doing those good works prepared for us in advance; run the race marked out for us. And just as for the homing pigeon, God has four methods or guidance systems through which this specific will for our lives is communicated.

Scripture. The Bible, together with other resources that reliably interpret its messages for us. Chapter 2 takes you through ways to use the Bible for personal guidance—and how to avoid misusing it.

Special Design. The way you are fearfully and wonderfully made. Chapter 3 shows how God can guide you through the use of the talents and gifts that make up your unique, God-given design, the kinds of environments in which you thrive, and the values and passions inherent in you.

Spirit. The loud-and-clear or still-and-small ways God speaks to us. God may or may not speak to you from a burning bush, but the Holy Spirit dwells inside of you and acts as Counselor to guide you. Chapter 4 takes a biblical look at how, when, and why God leads this way and how not to be misled in discerning whether the leadings are coming from God.

Circumstances. Open and closed doors. Chapter 5 outlines what the Bible really says about these signals of God's guidance and tells how to discover God's messages for you in the circumstances around you.

However, each of us has to make some very basic choices before God can lead us in any of these ways. First, *God has to be the Lord of our lives.* And God's lordship carries no authority with us unless it sometimes takes us places we don't want to go. Think of someone new joining the team at your workplace. You understand the big picture of how the place works; he or she doesn't. You know why things are done the way they are; the new employee doesn't. You let the new person ask questions, patiently showing him or her, more than once, how to do something, but you aren't looking for his or her advice the first day on the job. It's too early for a new employee to understand how such advice could improve anything.

In the same way, you can't improve on God's will for your life. You're new to the job, but God knows everything about how you operate best.

Second, *we have to hold lightly our own hopes and aspirations, remaining open to the possibility that God may be preparing something even better for us.* Perhaps you've heard that if you really want to make God laugh, begin listing all your plans. We simply can't see the big picture in the same way that God can, nor can we recognize all of the options, let alone define the right goals. James speaks harshly about the difference between dreaming with God and having your own aspirations.

> Now listen, you who say, "Today or tomorrow we will go to this or that city, spend a year there, carry on business and make money." Why, you do not even know what will happen tomorrow. What is your life? You are a mist that appears for a little while and then vanishes. Instead, you ought to say, "If it is the Lord's will, we will live and do this or that" (James 4:13-15).

It's okay to have dreams for your future—and some of them

may even come from God—but the trick is to have them without letting them possess you. If you aren't willing to relinquish them, you're in effect telling God, "I've got this all figured out, so I really don't need any help." To help us avoid this attitude, God often leaves the future a bit cloudy. That helps us remember that we are dependent on God, not on our own ability to plan and execute our ideas.

Third, *we have to nurture an openness to what God might be telling us.* In any endeavor, once you admit that you don't know where you're going, you can start asking for advice. When you're ready to look to God for guidance, you'll begin to notice signs, insights, and nuggets of wisdom that may have been there all along. Some of the guidance systems will sound more comfortable for you than others, but consider the true-life stories we've used to illustrate each system. If you don't *think* one will work for you, it probably won't! Ask God to show you more clearly how it operates, either through your own experiences or those of others, so you can be open to understanding the will of God.

Avoiding the Extremes

In the vast literature on the will of God, we can spot two extreme positions—and both of these positions can keep people from seeking guidance for their lives:

Extreme number one: God will always perfectly, obviously show you what you should do.

Some people hold that God leads so directly that you can always know with certainty what you are to do every moment of every day. People who hold this view might use phrases such as "I'm waiting for God to show me what to do" or "I'll move when I've got certain peace about this" or "God hasn't provided me with a sign yet." They may even pray over which socks to wear. However, if we ponder how desperately the disciples struggled to understand what Jesus wanted—even when he was right beside them—we can see that our own struggles are normal. We don't think they are a sign of immaturity or lack of faith.

We also don't think God can guide a stationary object, an apt description of what people can become if they wait for sure signs. Guidance, like many things, may first require action. If you're piloting a plane, it has to be moving through the air before many of the controls will work. When the aircraft is parked on the ground, the flaps, the rudder, the elevator, the ailerons, are useless. Unless you're flying the plane, you can't guide it. Similarly, God's guidance systems often don't function fully until you're moving out to do God's will. And further, expecting certainty often results in these traps:

A fear of flying. Some are afraid to seek God's will for their lives because they assume that it will be a sure path to misery. How often have you heard or thought to yourself, *But if I surrender my will, I'll end up in Africa as a missionary.* Or, *I'm a great artist/coach/teacher, but if I find out God's plans, I'll have to do something that doesn't fit so well with who I am.* Maybe you don't think you deserve fulfillment, or maybe you struggle to believe that God really wants what is best for you.

On the other hand, if you have set ideas on how using your gifts can best bring joy, you may not be open to God's ideas. What if Peter had said, "Nope, I'm a great fisherman. Surely God wants me to continue putting food on other people's tables." Or if David had said, "You don't understand, God. I'm the best shepherd in the country. Just a few more years and I'll be master of this whole spread. Leave it to be king? No way!" But they did listen to God, and were crucial in forming our understanding of our Creator. If God has another plan, we guarantee it is better than the best you can devise.

Doubting the instrument readings. In looking for guidance, we can become trapped by uncertainty. God doesn't want us to suffer paralysis of analysis as we check all of our choices— doing nothing doesn't even let us help fulfill God's general will for the world.

One person lamented, "I'm still uncertain whether going to nursing or medical school is the right choice. If either were *really* God's will for my life, wouldn't I know for sure?" If you hold your decisions to this standard, you are asking for more than most of the heroes of the Bible ever got. Remember, Isaac was named "Laughter" because Abraham and Sarah didn't only doubt, they *laughed* at God when told they would have a son in their old age. No matter how clear God was, people in the Bible still doubted. And God didn't always grant total assurance; in fact, when Moses was trying to identify the spirit speaking from the burning bush, God told him, "I will be with you. And this will be the sign to you that it is I who have sent you: When you have brought the people out of Egypt, you will worship God on this mountain" (Exodus 3:12).

In other words, Moses would only be *sure* it was God *after* he'd done everything God had asked of him. The assurance came after obedience, not before.

Depending on signal lights. These people are afraid to move without tangible proof of God's guidance. They say, "Ezekiel saw the wheel, Gideon saw the dew on the fleece, Peter saw Jesus— I'll just see what God wants me to do." This is true *if* God wants you to be the next Ezekiel or Gideon or Peter. You won't miss the signs. However, even in the lives of these great people of faith, such grand forms of guidance were rare. We'll show you how they used the other three guidance systems as well.

Expecting a smooth flight. People trapped by this misconception assume that troubles in life mean they missed God's direction. Being within the will of God doesn't mean success in worldly terms. Paul's epistles describe the Christian life as a fight or a race, not a stroll through the park. Flying on course has little to do with this world; we need to set our sights on the goals of the next.

Perhaps part of our modern-day anxiety about doing the will of God involves our impression that if things aren't going smoothly, we must be out of God's will. Past generations took

Jesus' words to heart: They knew they were going to have troubles and therefore didn't see them as "red lights." It was unusual to live to be seventy; most people succumbed to disease before turning forty-five. Industrial accidents were commonplace; there was no Department of Labor to enforce safety regulations. When tragedy was such an integral part of life, sometimes their goal was survival, getting through their own struggles with their faith intact. That tenacity of faith, not a lack of trouble, was their evidence of being in God's will.

While these fears can keep people from experiencing God's guidance, so can the opposite position.

Extreme number two: God has no specific plan for our lives.

Taking the other extreme, some people hold that there is no individual will for our lives. God gives us the general outlines, and as long as we stay within those guides we are on course. You might hear these people say things like "God gave us basic instructions and the brains to use them" or "The only source of guidance we have is the Bible—trusting anything else leaves you open to being misled by your own feelings." To us, this isn't consistent with the biblical picture of a God who numbers the hairs on our heads, who knows us before we are born, whose hand is inscribed with our names, who came to earth so we might have life and have it abundantly. But our position comes in part because of our understanding of God's will and who God is.

Receiving the gift of God's guidance is about living a worthy life, one that is full of fruit. God's ultimate goal for our lives isn't that we make something of ourselves, but that we become more like Christ. Being guided by God isn't like a train ride, where you get on at Point A, knowing the exact set of tracks the train will take to Point B. It's more like a bus ride. An infinite number of routes can eventually take you to Point B, although some are shorter or easier. Detours aren't necessarily bad. They may be a delightful side trip, just the preparation you need for the next stage of your journey. And, when you're traveling with God, your perception of the nature of Point B may change along the way.

No doubt you've been on one of those excursions where you set out with one purpose only to change goals midstream. God's guidance isn't always about knowing your destination. It isn't about success or safety from trials, but rather about carrying out the good works God planned for you while bearing fruit.

> For this reason, since the day we heard about you, we have not stopped praying for you and asking God to fill you with the knowledge of his will through all spiritual wisdom and understanding. And we pray this in order that you may live a life worthy of the Lord and may please him in every way: bearing fruit in every good work, growing in the knowledge of God, being strengthened with all power according to his glorious might so that you may have great endurance and patience, and joyfully giving thanks to the Father, who has qualified you to share in the inheritance of the saints in the kingdom of light. (Colossians 1:9-12)

Understanding God's will in this life will bring you knowledge, strength, endurance, and patience, all of which are necessary to get to the real goal of the heavenly crown.

The will of God for your life isn't a tiny bull's-eye you either hit or miss. One of Paul's favorite images for our lives is running a race in which all of us who finish can receive the crown of righteousness. Instead of worrying that finding God's will means discerning only one job, place to live, person to marry, or task to volunteer for, concentrate on getting in the right event, then crossing the finish line with everything that was entrusted to you. If our mistakes truly disqualified us, Paul himself would have been in deep trouble. If God's requirement was choosing right the first time, Paul's first "career" as the foremost persecutor of the church would have cut him off from ever being within the will of God. Instead, Paul tells us that he is an apostle of Christ Jesus by the *will of God*. (See Ephesians 1:1.)

God gives us another chance when we stray; God excels at using our mistakes to shape us for something good. Too many people avoid making decisions because they are afraid that if they choose wrongly, their life will be forever ruined. God doesn't work that way. Doing God's will is training for the race of faith to the best of our ability and then being a full participant: "Forgetting what is behind and straining toward what is ahead, I press on toward the goal to win the prize for which God has called me heavenward in Christ Jesus" (Philippians 3:13-14).

And as you go about living this worthy life, realize that you've already won the race. That's the freedom we have in Christ. That's what allowed Paul to put his past behind him. That's the attitude with which we can approach our finding God's will—we have the freedom to do our best. It's an adventure where we're guaranteed a safe ending, knowing that even if we somehow misstep, God will help us back on course.

Furthermore, you may not be off the course, but simply on one of those detours that will eventually work into God's plan. Some of these decisions aren't between right and wrong, but between good, better, and best. Some choices may cause us to work harder to reach God's goals, but you can still get there if you continue to press on.

Children in loving homes know that their chores are just part of living in the family. As long as they finish them, they have considerable freedom to choose what they do next. But if they haven't obeyed, they aren't free to do as they wish. That's where our freedom in Christ comes from, as well—when we assume the responsibilities of being a part of the body of Christ, we have the freedom to become all God meant for us to be.

God's will is in the details. If you're given a Herculean task, you might be more likely to ask for God's help. But God's will is in the little things as well as the major decisions of life. God doesn't want you waiting for the big moments to learn to seek guidance, for as Peter Marshall put it,

Jesus was being realistic about human life.
The truth is that our lives are made up of the sum of
the small decisions,
  the little turnings,
    the minute choices.
If we do not let God into these everyday details, practically
speaking we are not letting him in at all.[1]

The little things, of course, aren't necessarily easy—we're not talking about whether you have milk or orange juice with breakfast, but about how you make decisions when perhaps no one else will notice. They might include loving your neighbor, learning how to forgive, or doing things for the least of God's children. But they matter to God, just as how much manna the Israelites gathered in the wilderness mattered; whether Peter, John, and Andrew caught any fish; and whether one sheep was lost, even though ninety-nine others were safe.

Usually God asks for faith in little things to begin with. "Whoever can be trusted with very little can also be trusted with much, and whoever is dishonest with very little will also be dishonest with much" (Luke 16:10).

God isn't playing games with us. Finding God's will isn't like hide-and-seek or cat and mouse—it isn't a secret, but something God reveals to us if we're prepared to understand it. God's desire is for us to receive guidance, because we are God's friends.

> "I no longer call you servants, because a servant does not know his master's business. Instead, I have called you friends, for everything that I learned from my Father I have made known to you. You did not choose me, but I chose you and appointed you to go and bear fruit—fruit that will last" (John 15:15-16).

The will of God is a process, not a single purpose for your life. Few people can say, "I made it! I've found the will of God." We

---

[1] Peter Marshall, *Heaven Can't Wait* (Grand Rapids, Mich.: Chosen Books, 1963), 34.

continue to gain understanding and wisdom as we mature. And we continually seek God's guidance as our circumstances change and we discover even more good works God has prepared in advance for us to do.

Callings aren't only for ministers or missionaries. You can act on the will of God without doing it "professionally." Conversely, you can choose full-time ministry and still not be within God's purposes for *your* life. There is plenty of need for Christians in medical fields, in manufacturing, in classrooms— God only needs so many pastors and missionaries to nurture the body of Christ. The rest of us need to get out there and show the difference it makes in how we live.

It is far safer to follow God's plans, no matter how crazy they seem, than to follow your own desires. From Noah's ark building to Paul's shipwreck, from Abraham's near sacrifice of Isaac to the death and resurrection of Jesus, we see the truth of this statement. Isaiah, aware of Israel's imminent captivity in Babylon, prophesied, "This is what the Lord says—your Redeemer, the Holy One of Israel: 'I am the Lord your God, who teaches you what is best for you, who directs you in the way you should go. If only you had paid attention to my commands, your peace would have been like a river, your righteousness like the waves of the sea'" (Isaiah 48:17-18).

But to find that sort of peace, you have to trust God with your life.

Do You Trust God?

Behind Jane's house is a little pond that usually hosts a family of wood ducks in the springtime. Wood ducks tend to build their nests high up in trees; Jane's husband made a nesting box for them that can be seen from their back windows. The ducklings stay in the duck house when they're first born, safe from any predators. One day their mother or father tells them, "You're old enough to go out into the wide world. Today's the day you learn to swim!" Do they sail out of the nest, trusting their parent's wisdom?

Each one of them clings to the opening in the duck house for dear life until the cries and encouragement of their mother, already down below, convince them it's safe to leave the nest.

Do we trust God as much as those ducklings trust their mother?

At the heart of the four guidance systems is the truth that God loves us and dwells within us to guide us in the easiest way possible. Jesus told his disciples, "Those who love me will keep my word, and my Father will love them, and we will come to them and make our home with them" (John 14:23 NRSV).

You probably don't take advice from people you don't trust. You wouldn't invite them to live with you unless you trusted their goodness and character. Guidance isn't getting ordered around but willingly joining in the efforts of someone you believe in and love. Full freedom comes when you know the parameters within which it is safe to operate.

The pilots of the navy's precision flight team, the Blue Angels, practice and practice until they know the exact limits of their jets. As long as they honor what the craft will do, they can spin and dive and soar with safety. Similarly, this freedom of understanding what God wants us to do allows us to keep moving freely.

In fact, God lets us know that this is the case, telling us what we can expect:

> I will instruct you and teach you in the way you should go; I will counsel you and watch over you. Do not be like the horse or the mule, which have no understanding but must be controlled by bit and bridle or they will not come to you. (Psalm 32:8-9)

Actually, whether we choose to obey or ignore God's instructions is far more vital than whether or not a horse submits to training. If we choose to ignore the guidance we receive, we are free to go our own way. God won't rein us in. We can turn our backs and exercise free choice. We can either obey willingly or leave the corral. But if we leave, we're letting something else be lord of our lives. It might be money or prestige or simply fear.

Obedience means we're listening to a God who loves us unconditionally. If we truly understand that God wants the best for us, we can't help but obey out of love. Why would we flee from our Creator who knows exactly how to enrich our lives to the fullest?

Understanding God's Love

Saul never understood the love of God. He never grasped that God handpicked him to be king of Israel; all he had to do was follow instructions. The Bible tells us that Saul was the most handsome man in Israel, a head taller than anyone, the very image of a king. But he had absolutely no self-confidence. His first reaction when the prophet Samuel informed him that God had chosen him was "But I'm only from Benjamin, the smallest tribe in Israel, and my family is the least important of all the families of that tribe! Why are you talking like this to me?" (1 Samuel 9:21 NLT).

At first, one might think that Saul was merely being humble. Samuel reassured him that he really was fit to be king because Saul's own gifts and talents didn't matter. God would make him ready: "At that time the Spirit of the Lord will come upon you with power, and you will prophesy with them. You will be changed into a different person. After these signs take place, do whatever you think is best, for God will be with you" (1 Samuel 10:6-7 NLT).

Don't you wish God would guide you this clearly? That your vocation would be chosen for you and communion with the Spirit given to you? But Saul didn't understand that God loved him and Israel enough to do all of this for him. He didn't feel like a king. Some time later when Samuel assembled all of Israel for the coronation, no one could find the man of the hour. Their king was hiding in the baggage!

In his forty-two years as Israel's king, Saul never really got to know and trust God. He communicated to his Lord through

Samuel instead of seeking to understand God's desires directly. For a while, this worked fine. Saul simply waited for Samuel's counsel before making a move in battle or any other major decision. There eventually came a day, however, when Samuel was late. Or at least he was slower in arriving at the battlefield than Saul could tolerate. Despite all of the evidence over the years that the Lord was with him, Saul assumed that something had gone wrong, that he couldn't trust God or Samuel. And without looking to God for guidance, Saul went ahead and did what he thought was best, in the process deliberately breaking one of God's laws. To be fair, the king waited seven whole days for his prophet to arrive, but he then made his own sacrifice and burnt offering to God, something only the priests were allowed to do.

When Samuel arrived, he saw trouble at once:

> "How foolish!" Samuel exclaimed. "You have disobeyed the command of the Lord your God. Had you obeyed, the Lord would have established your kingdom over Israel forever. But now your dynasty must end, for the Lord has sought out a man after his own heart. The Lord has already chosen him to be king over his people, for you have not obeyed the Lord's command" (1 Samuel 13:13-14 NLT).

The man after God's own heart, of course, was David, who when he faced Goliath knew his strength would come from God. He looked to God whether he was afraid or uncertain or ecstatic. David wasn't perfect, but he constantly turned back to God, seeking forgiveness and new direction. During all the years David spent tending sheep and then running from Saul in the wilderness of Judea, he prayed and wrote psalms and got to know God.

Saul never did. The Bible paints a pitiful portrait of this once great king, troubled by evil spirits, devoured by jealousy, chasing away those closest to him, and finally dying with his sons on a battlefield. He never grasped what God wanted of him.

Saul never understood the God of whom the apostle Paul said,

> What, then, shall we say in response to this? If God is for us, who can be against us... For I am convinced that neither death

nor life, neither angels nor demons, neither the present nor
the future, nor any powers, neither height nor depth, nor anything else in all creation, will be able to separate us from the
love of God that is in Christ Jesus our Lord. (Romans 8:31, 38-
39)

We aren't obeying a God of fear, then, but a God of love.
Guidance isn't scary and uncertain, but rather trusting the
God who loves us completely.

The alternative to seeking God's guidance is relying on your
own devices. Think of some of the mistakes you've made in the
past if you need to convince yourself that God's plans are safer.
And then prepare your heart, soul, and mind to listen for God.

When Can We Count on Finding God's Will?

As we explore each of the four guidance systems, we'll look at
real examples of how people have used them to discover the will
of God in several areas.

In our work. While all big decisions are important, the subject of finding God's will for our lives is crucial in today's chaot-
ic workplace. Up until the past fifty years or so, the question of
God's will for one's life was two-dimensional: either you assumed
the role into which you were born or you were "called" to the
ministry as a priest, missionary, pastor, monk, or nun. People
inherited land or title, took over family trades, were apprenticed
to craftsmen for business reasons, or worked in the mines
because that was the only employment available in their region.
People didn't waste much time thinking about what they wanted to be when they grew up.

Now most of us have huge freedom to choose our futures, and
with that freedom comes the dilemma: how do we know what
God wants us to do? If we're going to put as much as two-
thirds of our lives into our work, most of us hope to find at least
some meaning and purpose at the office.

What if you're sure you know your field but can't find a job?
Or what if it seems you're on the road to success but suddenly

become one of the thousands of victims of downsizing? Or what if you feel dead-ended or find no joy in what you do? Did you choose the wrong career? Did you miss the divine plan? Consulting all four guidance systems can help you decide.

In our relationships. God isn't only concerned with our choices about marriage, but with our relationships with relatives and co-workers and fellow pilgrims in the church of Christ. And with how we choose our friends. Many of your relationships go smoothly without specific guidance. In others, you can learn to look to God.

In sufferings and challenges. We will say more than once and in more than one way that our concept of God doesn't include a cosmic being who sends tragedy to teach us a lesson. However, when our lives collide with the brokenness of the world, we can look to God for how to continue and how to respond.

In temptations. We are told that "God is faithful, and he will not let you be tested beyond your strength, but with the testing he will also provide the way out so that you may be able to endure it" (1 Corinthians 10:13 NRSV).

All of us at times have chosen not to resist temptation. God's guidance can help us avoid those traps.

For our maturity and development. God can show you where you most need to grow and how you might best go about it. Often these insights come as we learn to pay attention in new ways to what God might be saying.

For service to God and the rest of humankind. God wants you to find those good works prepared in advance for you to do. These works come in all shapes and sizes and may be here or far away.

Experiencing the gift of God's guidance for all these areas in your life requires constant attention to God. You can make it easier by surrounding yourself with others who also want to rely on God's guidance. That doesn't mean getting together to second-guess every decision, but benefiting from the experiences of others who are striving to find the fulfilling life God has in mind.

You could say that birds have it easier than we do since they don't question the guidance systems they're using. It's all instinct. Yet the more we use God's guidance systems, the more we trust that what we are discerning is the right course. Checking their validity becomes second nature. We know the Bible and its timeless standards. We have friends who are wise and who hold us accountable. We know ourselves and what we do well. We recognize the input of the Holy Spirit. We've practiced weighing these things against the circumstances in which we find ourselves. It's almost as if we're flying on auto-pilot—the systems function without our constant, conscious checking.

But it isn't really being on auto-pilot—it's turning the command controls over to God instead of obsessing over every instrument reading. It's building that relationship with God so that the laws are written on our hearts where we can't miss them.

God values us substantially more than the pigeons and geese and provides even more guidance for our journey home toward heaven. If we take the time to understand the four ways in which we are guided and how to integrate them, we, too, can stay on course.

Let the morning bring me word of your unfailing love,
for I have put my trust in you.
Show me the way I should go,
for to you I lift up my soul.
Teach me to do your will,
for you are my God;
may your good Spirit lead me on level ground.
—Psalm 143:8, 10

Reflections for Your Own LifeDirections

As you work through these chapters, **keep a journal of your reflections on each chapter.**

Make your answers to these reflection suggestions as long or as short as you like, but take the time to apply what you are reading to your own life as you proceed.

1. Look through our main points in this chapter. Which one caught your attention the most? Why?
   - The true goal of finding God's guidance is to become more and more like Christ.
   - God still speaks to help us translate the general principles contained in Scripture into the good works God has in mind for us.
   - God's guidance systems only function when God is the Lord of our lives.
   - God's will isn't a bull's-eye or a road map, but a process, a light to our path.
   - We can receive God's guidance when we love and trust that God has the absolute best in mind for us.

2. When, if ever, have you felt guided by God? Or, if that hasn't happened, what do you think of when the topic of God's guidance comes up?

3. Think of a major life decision you have made: your career, your marriage, a major purchase—such as a home. How did you make that decision? How did you seek God's will? What "practical" criteria did you use? Try to remember the process you went through. Then, as you read through the next four chapters, we'll ask you to compare that process with how you might proceed using *Scripture,* your *special design,* the *Spirit,* and *circumstances.*

4. When have you looked for God's guidance and felt that none was forthcoming? What kind of guidance had you hoped to receive? Record your thoughts.

5. We noted that according to Jesus, doing God's will is our source of food, joy, and family. How does this hold true in your life?

6. Are you more like Saul (who didn't believe God loved him) or David? Read Psalm 139. What verses can make God's love seem more real to you?

Guidance System #1

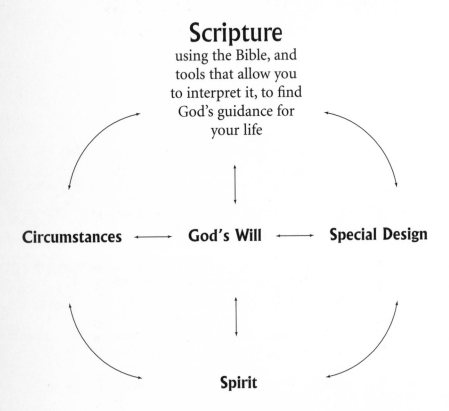

Scripture
using the Bible, and
tools that allow you
to interpret it, to find
God's guidance for
your life

Circumstances   **God's Will**   **Special Design**

Spirit

Chapter 2

What Has God Already Told Us?
Finding Guidance Through Scripture

I have hidden your word in my heart
that I might not sin against you.

—Psalm 119:11

Before you read this chapter, think about:

1. How would you rank your comfort with finding God's guidance through Scripture? Use a scale of 1 ("I'm not sure if this works") to 10 ("I'm very comfortable with this form of God's guidance").

2. How do you think this piece of God's system for finding God's will works best? What questions do you have about it?

3. What are your biggest worries or fears about using Scripture to find God's guidance for your life?

Homing pigeons don't hesitate in midair. They don't debate with each other. They don't circle while they decide which way to go or what route to take. And they never have to think about which of their four built-in guidance systems to use. Instinctively, pigeons employ what is most appropriate at any given moment: the position of the sun during the day, the magnetic pull of the earth when it's overcast, their eyesight if they can see their loft, and so on.

At least some of our decisions can be almost that instinctive, because we can train ourselves to know God's best source of guidance for the question we ask. We won't make decisions by instinct but by the knowledge and wisdom we gain from the Holy Spirit's training in using these systems. We'll still spin in circles occasionally—especially over some of life's most complex decisions—but we can shorten the duration of those holding patterns when we know which guidance system to use.

We believe the Bible is the guidance system we should turn to first, because it's the operating manual provided by the one who created us. You wouldn't dream of flying a jet without understanding the instrument panel—the purpose of each dial, switch, and control. The fact is, you can't even practice piloting a plane without taking classes and studying the manuals. If we take that attitude toward the Bible, we give Scripture its proper place as we search for God's guidance.

The Bible, simply put, is our primary source of wisdom—an operating manual for human beings full of directions for applying God's ideals to our everyday lives. Just as instructions let you know how to fly a plane or put together a bike, computer, or stereo, the Bible provides us with guidelines for how we can fulfill God's purposes. There isn't much point in looking for other sources of wisdom until we've tried to answer our questions and concerns with the clear insights already provided in Scripture.

Unfortunately, there are two kinds of people in the world: those who read instructions before they start a project and those who read them only after they come to their wit's end as to how to proceed. It is no wonder that many of us fail to look at the clearest source of God's will for our lives. Yet even if we do, we may struggle to put to use a book written so long ago to people whose circumstances were so different from ours.

Some people try to use the Bible like a crystal ball. Hannah Smith tells of a woman of integrity who stole some money after she opened her Bible at random and put her finger on "All things are yours" (1 Corinthians 3:21).

Other people fail to study properly the message of a complicated Bible passage. As a mother broke up a fight between her two preschoolers, she said, "There's no excuse for hitting each other. How could you?"

"But Mom, I was just doing what the Bible says—you know, do to others as they do to you."

People also fall into the trap of approaching the Bible with a preconceived notion of the truth, closed to a more accurate, more helpful interpretation. Galileo unjustly spent the last eight years of his life under house arrest because he dared to "contradict" the Scriptures (and the religious authorities) with his claim that the earth revolved around the sun.

Historically, though, people *have* found specific guidance in Scripture passages that bore good fruit for their lives, sometimes through a single verse. St. Augustine, struggling with his own weaknesses, was praying when he sensed that God was commanding him to pick up his Bible and read. He renewed his commitment to God after opening the New Testament at random to the words "Rather, clothe yourselves with the Lord Jesus Christ, and do not think about how to gratify the desires of the sinful nature" (Romans 13:14).

Martin Luther began the Protestant Reformation after grasping for himself the meaning of "For we hold that a person is justified by faith apart from works prescribed by the law" (Romans 3:28 NRSV).

An early missionary about to give up on translating the Bible into a particularly difficult tribal language was able to continue successfully after he read at random, "There was given him that…all languages should serve him" (Daniel 7:14 KJV).

George Mueller found inspiration to build his fourth and fifth homes for orphans, despite no guaranteed funding, in "Commit to the Lord whatever you do, and your plans will succeed" (Proverbs 16:3). His financial needs were met through donations without his doing any soliciting.

In other words, although people have misused the Bible to support their own selfish desires or grave misunderstandings, people have also used the Bible to find guidance that takes them to the center of God's will. Quite frankly, the Bible is a deep, wise, and sometimes misused book. There is profound wisdom in Karl Barth's statement that he took the Bible far too seriously to take it literally—or even in Mark Twain's comment that it was what he *did* understand in the Bible that frightened him. Open to certain places and you might find justification for slavery, war, the oppression of women, or even that the heavens revolve around the earth—*if* you misuse God's Word or isolate its messages from other sources of God's wisdom.

But *anyone can learn* to use the Bible.

If you're one of the millions of people who have already invested the time and energy to learn how to access the wisdom of the Bible, you'll find in this chapter some succinct reminders of how to use Scripture wisely to find God's will. And if you're still unsure how to plow through the narrative accounts and dietary laws it contains to find God's message for you, we hope to point you in the right direction.

First, pause for a moment. Ask yourself what messages you think the Bible contains. Your answer may depend on your view of God.

- If you think of our Creator as an authority figure ready to prosecute you for minor infractions, you may think of Scripture as a compilation of do's and don'ts. With this view, the Bible becomes a yardstick for measuring failure.

- However, if you believe the Bible exists because God loves us, the guidance it contains takes on an entirely different cast. Then it becomes the wisdom of our Creator, instructions inspired by the one who knows best how we should live and work and celebrate our existence. Jesus pointed out, "You search the scriptures because you think that in them you have eternal life; and it is they that testify on my behalf" (John 5:39 NRSV).

Whether you devote hours each week to Bible study or try with what little time you have to grasp its main points, the most important goal is that you grow closer to God.

The Importance of Your Relationship With God

Why get closer to God? Because the deeper your relationship with God, the better you'll understand how to look to the authority of the Bible. "But, as it is written, 'What no eye has seen, nor ear heard, nor the human heart conceived, what God has prepared for those who love him'—these things God has revealed to us through the Spirit; for the Spirit searches everything, even the depths of God" (1 Corinthians 2:9-10 NRSV).If you accept that God loves you, then God can reveal to you the wisdom of the Bible through the Spirit.

The more you're around someone, the more you understand what they want. Best friends can laugh with each other over a single word. Couples who have been married for years sometimes don't even need *one* word to know what the other is thinking. The more you invest in a relationship—not only spending time with a person but trying to understand him or her as well—the better it gets.

A major role of the Bible is to help us understand our relationship with God. The more you value that relationship, the more you'll want to discover God's character as revealed in the Scripture, thus deepening your relationship. And the deeper the relationship, the more you'll understand the Bible.

Approaching the Bible

The Bible uses many types of literature to convey truth: song, story, allegory, poetry, history, riddle, and more. While some guidance from the Bible is straightforward, in other passages it's hard to grasp what message there might be for you personally. Whatever the format, though, every section contains truths. As a simple illustration, look at the first chapter of Genesis.

Millions of people around the world were convinced of the truth of the Creation story on Christmas Eve, 1968. If you're too young to have experienced that moment, try to recreate it for yourself. Find a photograph of the earth taken from outer space and ponder its beauty. Then imagine your awe as the cameras from Apollo 8 relayed back to earth the *first* pictures we had ever seen of fragile earth. Add to that the stirring first four verses of Genesis, the words Col. Frank Borman read as our luminous planet rose up out of the darkness:

> In the beginning God created the heaven and the earth. And the earth was without form, and void; and darkness was upon the face of the deep. And the spirit of God moved upon the face of the waters. And God said, Let there be light: and there was light. And God saw the light, that it was good. (KJV)

Isn't it true that our planet is a miracle? An amazing refuge for life in the vastness of the heavens? When we read the Bible as a storehouse of wisdom, we find a God who created a world full of beauty and wonder to serve as our home, who wants the best for us, who forgives us no matter how many times we turn away, and who provides guidance for how to best live in this life. Try to read the Bible—whether the section before you is poetry, strange tales of war, or difficult prophecies—with a heart for the truths God wants to convey to you.

Searching for God's guidance isn't a burden we carry, forcing us to read the Bible endlessly. Instead, it's the sure path to freedom that enables us to obey God. It takes away the load of managing ourselves and dealing with our guilt. The Bible is full of promises about the richness of life when God is in control and the Scriptures are honored. The book of Proverbs gives the value of such wisdom:

> If you accept my words
> and treasure up my commandments within you...
> if you indeed cry out for insight, and raise your voice for
>   understanding;
> if you seek it like silver,
>   and search for it as for hidden treasures—
> then you will...find the knowledge of God...
> Then you will understand righteousness and justice and
>   equity, every good path;
> for wisdom will come into your heart...
> understanding will guard you.
> (Proverbs 2:1-11, selected verses NRSV)

The Bible, then, isn't a sourcebook of "Thou shalt nots" but one of treasure for our lives. What if we searched the Bible as we would a field with hidden treasure? We would find a treasure that

- can teach, reprove, correct, and train us for righteousness so that everyone who belongs to God may be proficient, equipped for every good work. (See 2 Timothy 3:16-17.)
- can transform us by the renewing of our minds so we can discern the will of God—what is good and acceptable and perfect. (See Romans 12:2.)
- can provide blessing when we put into action what we know to be true about the law. (See James 1:25.)
- can help us live without fear. (See Proverbs 1:33.)

With those key concepts in mind, you can begin to navigate the Bible, a volume so rich and fascinating that civilization has drawn new insights and lessons from it for almost three thousand years. *Knowing* those concepts, however, is inadequate apart from a commitment to *live* the clear truths of Scripture. We can learn from Solomon's mistake, supposedly one of the wisest people ever to live.

Solomon the Wise

At the beginning of Solomon's kingship, God offered him any-thing he wanted—and Solomon asked for discernment and wis-dom so he could be a good ruler. God was so impressed with this unselfish request that Solomon also received "riches, pos-sessions, and honor, such as none of the kings had who were before you, and none after you shall have the like" (2 Chroni-cles 1:12 NRSV).

The Bible describes the wisdom of Solomon as

> vast as the sand on the seashore, so that Solomon's wisdom surpassed the wisdom of all the people of the east, and all the wisdom of Egypt. He was wiser than anyone else...his fame spread throughout all the surrounding nations. He com-posed three thousand proverbs, and his songs numbered a thousand and five. He would speak of trees, from the cedar that is in the Lebanon to the hyssop that grows in the wall; he would speak of animals, and birds, and reptiles, and fish. People came from all the nations to hear the wisdom of Solomon; they came from all the kings of the earth who had heard of his wisdom. (1 Kings 4:29-34 NRSV)

Yet despite his vast knowledge, his ability to cut to the quick of a matter requiring judgment, and the capacity he had to con-vey this wisdom to others, Solomon somehow lost sight of the basic wisdom God gives to all of us—the written Scriptures—and married foreign wives.

You don't have to have the proverbial wisdom of Solomon to understand what God repeatedly told Israel: If you marry peo-ple who worship other gods, eventually you will forsake me and look to these other gods as well. God said as much in Exo-dus 34:15; in Deuteronomy 7:3-4; and in Joshua 23:12-13. And what happened to Solomon when he disobeyed? Those foreign wives influenced him to build altars and temples to other gods and he lost his full devotion to the one true God. The result? The end of the united kingdom of Israel. God made it clear that failing to worship the one true God caused the loss of the kingdom for Solomon's son.

Before you panic and think that you have to memorize the entire Bible, note that Solomon need only have looked at the first of the Ten Commandments to avoid his downfall: "You shall have no other gods before me." Jesus made the Ten even easier when he said, "Love the Lord your God with all your heart, and with all your soul, and with all your mind. This is the greatest and first commandment. And a second is like it: "'You shall love your neighbor as yourself'" (Matthew 22:37–39 NRSV).

To find God's guidance in the Bible, keep the following principles in mind. We'll consider each one individually:

- Clarify what you are asking of the Bible.
- Consider what the whole Bible has to say on a subject— view the trajectory of Scripture.
- Determine whether your question concerns a disputable or nondisputable matter.
- Check your interpretations with those of others in community.

Clarify what you are asking of the Bible. To get started using the Bible to find guidance, clarify in your own mind the questions you are asking. Are you looking for rules or values to apply consistently in day-to-day issues of right and wrong? For wisdom in selecting something of more general direction, such as a career? Or for a specific answer to a specific problem or situation? Then consider whether the Bible is the best guidance system to use.

Let's take marriage, for example. The Bible gives us broad guidelines, including:

- Marry someone who shares your faith. (2 Corinthians 6:14)
- Marriage is honorable, and the marriage bed is to be kept pure. (Hebrews 13:4)
- Unmarried people are likely to have more time to devote to Christian service. (1 Corinthians 7:32)

Thus, you could use the Bible to understand God's purposes for marriage. Further study would help you gain insights about your own maturity and readiness. You could also study the biblical view of marriage with your future mate.

The Bible, though, may or may not provide specifics—like telling you whether to marry Sally or Sue (or Steve or Stan). One seminary professor relates that no less than six men came to him one week convinced that the Bible had told them exactly whom to marry. Of course, they all wanted the hand of the same woman!

You are *always* safe in using the Bible to establish your moral principles, including those that will help you make decisions about marriage—and we will suggest a process to follow. However, once you've put the ground rules in place, it's time to look to the other systems to balance out what your heart is telling you—as we'll show in the next chapters.

Does this mean you should *never* ask specific questions of the Bible? That it only provides general principles? We know that the experiences of others testify differently. People often receive direct guidance while reading Scripture—above we cited St. Augustine, Martin Luther, and George Mueller. However, most commonly, they weren't *looking* for answers to a specific question as they read. Instead, they were *listening* to what God had to say to them.

While we *won't* say that God can never lead when someone opens the Bible and points to a certain verse (although we wish them luck if they open to the Song of Songs or the genealogies contained in the Old Testament), we do know it won't always work.

Perhaps you've heard about the young parents who opened and pointed to find a name for their first child. That boy has struggled ever since trying to fit Wonderful Counselor, Mighty God, Everlasting Father, Prince of Peace in those little spaces on applications.

Or the teenager who couldn't decide which dress to wear to the prom. She opened the Bible and read "Pretend you are in mourning. Dress in mourning clothes, and don't use any cosmetic lotions. Act like a woman who has spent many days grieving for the dead" (2 Samuel 14:2). Puzzled, she tried again and read, "Trust in the Lord with all your heart and lean not on your own understanding" (Proverbs 3:5).

God may be able to reach us even when we're unsure how to
find wisdom, but why make it harder? We can guarantee the
effectiveness of another way to seek guidance from the Bible.

First, get to know the Bible before you need specific answers.
Its core message is how God operates and seeks to establish a
relationship with us.

Second, find regular times to read and study that suit you. You
might take a class, buy a study guide, read with a friend, listen
to Scripture on tape. Find some way that appeals to you.

Third, digest the Bible in small bites. Read just a few verses.
Pause before you bite off any more. Does God wish you to
gain any insights for your own life from this passage?

A young man named Mark Bouman faced a major decision:
whether or not to become a missionary to the strife-torn country of Cambodia. During his daily Bible study (not during a specific search for an answer), he read, then reread Jonah 4:11,
describing the Ninevites as "people who cannot tell their right
hand from their left." Mark thought, *What an apt description
of Cambodians.* Twenty years of Pol Pot's rule had left most of
Cambodia illiterate and in poverty. Few knew of God. And the
millions of land mines left over from war literally took the
right or left hand of thousands of people each year.

Mark didn't accept this insight alone as guidance. The next
morning in church, however, the head of the missionary organization Mark hoped to join read from the same text and said,
"This describes the Cambodians. We need to help them learn
their right hand from their left." Mark points to this "coincidence" as a major factor in getting his attention to seriously consider going to Cambodia. To make his final decision, though, he
looked for confirmation from the other guidance systems. He
felt led by his wife's equal zeal for their calling, the circumstances
that helped him meet the rigorous requirements of the organization he joined, and the ways his gifts and talents qualified him
for the undertaking.

While not all experiences match Mark's, he put into practice
a sound method for using the Bible.

- He was familiar with it; he studied and read it regularly. Mark had been praying about the decision to go to Cambodia for some time, but wasn't pondering that question as he read this particular passage. That's one of the most important aspects of using the Bible for guidance: read it frequently with an ear to what God might be saying to you.
- He tried to listen for God as he read, using a technique often described as "praying the Scripture." Read slowly, staying with a short passage until you sense whether God wants to speak to you through that passage. If so, turn the passage into prayer.
- When Mark thought he'd received an answer, he waited for confirmation from other sources and discussed his interpretation with his wife and others. He didn't jump to the conclusion that God had guided his decision.

God *can* guide us very specifically through the Bible, opening our eyes wide as we read a passage or even a single verse. But Mark already knew that the choice he was considering was within the moral will of God as outlined in the Bible. We are to take the good news of Jesus to others. Mark was now trying to decide how he *specifically* was meant to carry out Christ's command. And he didn't rely only on the verse that had caught his attention. He looked for guidance from the other systems.

Thus, if you are seeking guidance for a specific question, while God can use the Bible to guide you, you may want to first look at the general principles, continue to pray, and start checking the other systems. However, in determining those general principles, look at all of the messages the Bible has about that subject, and not a single passage. Bible verses are seldom meant to be read in isolation: often not only is the context of the verse important but what the scope of the Bible has to say about the theme of the verse. That's the next principle of reading the Bible for guidance.

Consider what the whole Bible has to say on a subject.
People tend to fall into three basic groups in how they use Scripture. Picture the Bible for a moment as a river tour of the Grand Canyon, with different terrains, rocks exposed from different geological periods, and an infinite variety of water conditions, with hazards and channels marked by buoys.

One method of navigating the Bible is to tie yourself to particular verses, as you would to a single buoy in a river. Your position is secure and sure. But if you stay in one place, you can't see the majesty of the rest of the journey or learn from how things change. For example, when medieval people tied themselves to "Thou shalt not suffer a witch to live," overlooking "Thou shalt not kill," the result was the brutal witch hunts that continued for centuries.

Sometimes people use this method out of a longing to turn gray areas into black-and-white certainties. Over and over Jesus warned against this. Whenever the Pharisees tried to tie Jesus to a single buoy, he changed the course completely. An eye for an eye? No, turn the other cheek. Stone a woman caught in adultery? Only if you've never sinned. Forgive someone seven times? No, seventy times seven. And so on. Instead of tying the law to a single verse (and without contradicting the verses to which the Pharisees pointed), Jesus deepened, expanded, or reinterpreted the passage. The individual laws, according to Jesus, seem to only hint at what God really has in mind for us.

While living by a principle a single verse contains—especially a commandment—may be fine, making decisions based on a single verse with no other input may be dangerous. Before doing the latter, consider the context of the verse and whether it contradicts any principles found elsewhere in Scripture.

Another method is to add *to* the Bible, tossing your own buoys into the water. People reading Scripture from this point of view don't consider the Bible to be God's final revelation to us, which allows them to consult many other sources of wisdom. True, the world is full of experts and sources of authoritative wisdom. But there's a difference between using those sources to gain additional insight versus disregarding the Bible's ultimate authority in favor of their view. People often resort to this method to turn matters that are clearly black and white within Scripture into gray.

In the early church, a group called the Gnostics were convinced that everything in the world was evil and that our bodies were prisons from which the soul longed to escape. Some of them tended toward asceticism—severe discipline of their bodies—while others thought they could use their bodies to sin as much as they wanted. *All* of them ignored Scriptures such as "The earth is the Lord's, and everything in it, the world, and all who live in it" (Psalm 24:1) or "Do you not know that your body is a temple of the Holy Spirit, who is in you, whom you have received from God?" (1 Corinthians 6:19). They didn't listen to the Bible's teaching that our bodies and the world God made are good.

The danger is putting other books or experts on a par with the Bible. The Bible needs to remain the standard for measuring unchangeable truth.

The final method looks at a theme or issue within the entire teaching or trajectory of Scripture, as you might travel the length of a river before drawing conclusions about the trip. Instead of tying an interpretation to one verse, this method discerns how an issue is handled in the books of the Law, the Prophets, the Gospels, the Epistles, and finally in Revelation.

This last method ensures that we pick up the authentic message of the Bible. It helps us understand which matters are black and white and which are tougher, gray issues requiring that we balance competing principles. This method requires that you know enough about the Bible to trace the Bible's message, but you don't have to be a biblical scholar. With all of the tools that exist today, much of the work has been done for you. You can read through several translations to find one that uses language you can understand. Many editions contain notes that explain unfamiliar words or customs. There are books that summarize the central messages of the Bible as well as collections of verses that highlight what the Bible has to say about specific topics or problems in life.

To illustrate the tools you might use, let's take the topic of the Sabbath—how are we to observe this day that God set apart for rest? You might use:

- A topical Bible—a reference volume that lists Scripture verses by topic (even though a verse might not contain a specific word). If you look up the word "Sabbath," you'll find references to verses that describe the history of the Sabbath, from its institution at Creation to Jesus' teachings on keeping the Sabbath. You can also read specific regulations for observing the Sabbath. From this survey, you'll discover that the Old Testament understanding that no work could be done on the Sabbath was reinterpreted after Jesus remarked, "The Sabbath was made for man, not man for the Sabbath" (Mark 2:27).

- A concordance—an index that lists all occurrences of a word in the Bible. If you look up the word *Sabbath* you'll find, for example, that it occurs 134 times in the New International Version of the Bible. The final reference, in Hebrews, reminds us that if God needed a day of rest, so do we.

- Cross references—many Bibles "chain reference" key subjects, telling you in footnotes or margin notes where else in the Bible you can learn more on a subject. *The New Scofield Study System* lists six different cross references for Jesus' statement in Mark 2:27 that the Sabbath was made for man and not man for the Sabbath. Ezekiel 20:12, for example, tells that one of the functions of the Sabbath is to remind Israel that God made them holy.

- Commentaries—reference works that compile knowledge or provide insights about biblical passages. Some of the most accessible to nonscholars are *Barclay's Daily Study Bible* volumes or the Bible study guides in the *Mastering the Basics* series from Serendipity House, which are designed for small group study. You can also use a single-volume study Bible such as the NIV *Study Bible* or *Life*

Application® Bible. One way to choose a commentary for your own library or repeated use is to look up the same passage in several references: Which one gives you the most helpful information?

• Software programs—Computer software packages combine many or all of the features of concordances, topical Bibles, and commentaries. These programs make understanding a given topic fast and easy, and the packages vary in price to meet many budget needs.

You needn't have all of these to guarantee your understanding of a biblical topic. Try out several at a library to see which is easiest for you to use. Yet before you limit your study to just one or two of these aids to understanding the Bible, make sure you know their limitations. In most cases, someone's made choices about which verses are included in indexes and references and they may be biased by his or her own viewpoints. You decrease the risk of being tied to their agendas by using more than one source or research technique.

Determine whether your question concerns a disputable or nondisputable matter. Once you discover what the Bible has to say about a topic, your next step in finding guidance through the Bible is separating disputable from nondisputable matters. As you use the above tools, what do you discover? Was what you read consistent? On many topics, the Bible never alters its message. No stealing, no worshiping other gods, watch out for the poor, widowed, and sick—these are just a few of the nondisputable directives God gave us. Like it or not, we were handed the Ten Commandments, not the Ten Recommendations.

In contrast, some themes change, develop, and modify throughout the Bible. Our relationship to the Sabbath and the role of dietary laws, circumcision, and sacrifice all change by the end of the New Testament.

Still other subjects are so complex that we will always struggle to comprehend what God wants us to do. The answers for these intricate matters may even be inconsistent within the Bible. No, this isn't blasphemy but fact. Paul tells us to obey those in authority, yet we know God honored Daniel for disobeying the edicts of King Nebuchadnezzar. Even though Proverbs tells us over and over that the wicked will perish, we often see the righteous persecuted. We are told not to kill, but after this commandment the Bible contains story upon story of God helping the Israelites wage war against their enemies. This area is so complex that in Christian history at least four distinct perspectives on war and our response to war have arisen, each based on different passages of the Bible. These kinds of apparent contradictions require study of their context and intended audiences.

Finally, on certain subjects, the Bible tells us to make up our own minds based on our own circumstances and the strength of our faith. Paul devoted a whole chapter of the Book of Romans to admonishing us to "accept him whose faith is weak, without passing judgment on disputable matters" (Romans 14:1). Paul then lists all sorts of disputable matters concerning eating meat, when to worship, and other things that aren't essential to our belief in Jesus Christ.

Try to determine the category into which your question falls. If you read, "Thou shalt not…" in Leviticus, in Proverbs, in the Prophets, in Matthew, and in Timothy—if the Bible gives the same message through hundreds of years and vastly different settings—the matter isn't disputable. If Jesus or the apostles reinterpret the Law for us, we can trust the position taken in the New Testament. Those are the easy areas in which to find God's will.

You have the freedom, in other words, to decide within the general wisdom of Scripture and your spiritual needs. To return to our example, determining the day on which we honor the Sabbath is specifically listed by Paul as a disputable matter (Romans 14:5). When things are disputable, you can apply a series of principles to determine what you should do:

1. God gives you the freedom to decide your position on these matters. As Paul says, "Some judge one day to be better than another, while others judge all days to be alike. Let all be fully convinced in their own minds. Those who observe the

day, observe it in honor of the Lord" (Romans 14:5-6 NRSV).

The bigger principle in this verse is that it is possible for Christians to take opposite positions on such matters and still be within the will of God for their individual lives.

2. The impact on your own faith is your guide in choosing your position. Maybe always attending worship on Sundays helps you set aside time for God in a way that sets the tone for the rest of the week. Maybe you do best when each week you choose between two or three options for your day of rest and worship.

3. Your decision in disputable matters applies only to you. "So whatever you believe about these things," the Bible says, "keep between yourself and God" (Romans 14:22).

We aren't to pass judgment on people who take a different position. In other words, don't sweat the small stuff.

4. Whatever your position, you may need to alter your behavior when you're with others if your normal path might cause them to stumble. Perhaps your spouse or prayer partners find it too easy to disregard their spiritual life without the anchor of Sunday worship. In that case, God asks you to join with them.

5. Strive to be at peace even in diversity of opinion on such matters, "for the kingdom of God is not a matter of eating and drinking, but of righteousness, peace and joy in the Holy Spirit" (Romans 14:17). Paul knew what he was talking about here. How often do people outside the church ridicule us by saying, "How can they have the answers when they can't even agree about drinking wine or grape juice?"

Check your interpretations with those of others in community. And that's one of the big messages of the Bible— unity. We're supposed to get along even as we struggle to understand the Bible. Its complexity testifies to the truth that most of the issues we face have no simple answers.

One way to test your own interpretations is to study with other people. The essential principles of our faith, contained in documents such as the Nicene Creed, were worked out in community. In contrast, many cults take as foundational teachings one person's interpretations of Scripture, closed to questioning, which the leader developed in isolation from others.

While we can learn much from past scholars, each generation also needs to take a look at its blind spots and determine where it has misinterpreted Scripture. A good example would be the nineteenth-century debate over slavery. In biblical times slavery was commonplace. For generations, good Bible-thumping slave-owners justified their classification of slaves as property, not humans, through Genesis 9:25. This verse follows the strange story of Noah's sons finding their father quite drunk. Shem and Japheth backed into the tent with a covering on their shoulders so as to cover their father without seeing his nakedness, this after Ham, the father of Canaan, had gazed at Noah. When Noah woke up and heard what Ham had done, he said, "Cursed be Canaan! The lowest of slaves shall he be to his brothers." Slave owners then pointed to rules about slave ownership, from Leviticus through the teachings of Paul, assuming that if the Bible told them how to own a slave, it must be okay to own them.

Over hundreds of years people slowly began to realize that in God's eyes slaves were no different than themselves. Different verses in the Bible took precedence, such as "There is neither Jew nor Greek, slave nor free, male nor female, for you are all one in Christ Jesus" (Galatians 3:28). Slowly, as people shared their insights, many Christians began to work toward the abolition of slavery.

Interpretations will change—often it is imperative that they do. For centuries, humankind interpreted our being given dominion over all the earth (in the first chapter of Genesis) as a license to do what we wished to this planet and the other living things with which we share it. In recent decades Christians in community have reinterpreted our dominion as *stewardship* of the earth. After all, "The earth is the *Lord's,* and everything in it, the world, and all who live in it" (Psalm 24:1, emphasis added). We need the wisdom of those around us to test our ideas.

In the same way, how we understand elements of Bible stories changes. Take the story of the Prodigal Son. Knowing that in first-century Jewish culture when the younger son asked for his inheritance he was wishing his father were already dead, makes the father's forgiveness even more powerful. The more input we have from others, whether from commentaries, Bible study groups, computer software, or great teachers, the more we can learn about God's will for our lives.

Not one of us—not even the greatest biblical scholar (remember Solomon?)—will always get it right. When you stumble, you can again turn to the Bible. Not only will you find lots of company, but you'll discover one more universal truth essential to grasp if you are seeking God's will: *No matter how badly you stumble, God stands ready to forgive once you admit your wrong and ask for forgiveness.*

The disciples missed your messages
* but you were patient with them.*
People sought the wrong kind of Messiah,
* so you taught about your kingdom.*
The lawyer didn't recognize his neighbor,
* and you began, "A man was going down from*
*   Jerusalem to Jericho…."*
On the road to Emmaus, your companions pondered
*   an empty tomb,*
* and you showed them truths from Moses to the*
*   Prophets.*
The words of Isaiah baffled the Ethiopian,
* so you whisked Philip right to his chariot.*
I'm not the first to struggle.
Guide me, too, as I seek the treasures of your Word.
* Amen.*

Reflections for Your Own LifeDirections

1. Look through our main points in this chapter. Which one caught your attention the most? Why?
   - The Bible is our instruction manual for living as part of God's kingdom. To use it we need to
     (a) clarify what we are asking of the Bible;
     (b) consider what the whole Bible has to say on a subject;
     (c) determine whether our question concerns a disputable or nondisputable matter;
     (d) check our interpretations with those of others in community.
   - While people find guidance from reading single verses, the more you read the Bible, the more opportunities God has to guide you through it.
   - The Bible contains gray areas as well as black-and-white truths. God says that it is sometimes okay to disagree.

2. Looking back to the major decision you recorded in chapter 1, did you over- or under-utilize this guidance system in making that decision? What might you do differently?

3. Did you agree or disagree with our approach of navigating the entirety of Scripture before discerning what the Bible has to say on any topic? Why or why not? Where would you struggle in this process?

4. Try "praying the Scriptures" this week. Journal about your insights or what God might be trying to tell you as you read key verses for this chapter:
Proverbs 2:1-11
Romans 14
Psalm 119:33-40, 89-104
James 1:5-8

5. If you struggle finding time for regular Bible study, which one of these methods might work for you? Make a commitment to yourself to try it for the next month (some experts say it takes just thirty days to form a habit).

- Join or form a small group. Choose a study method and hold each other accountable.
- Choose a book or magazine of devotions to read regularly.
- Set aside time to listen to a favorite Bible teacher on the radio.
- Choose an author you like to follow. Set aside time for reading his or her books.
- Purchase Bible audiotapes or borrow them from the library. Listen to them in the car or while doing regular tasks (mowing the lawn, washing dishes, etc.).
- Choose a book of the Bible that appeals to you. Read a few verses each day and journal about what they mean to you.

Experiencing God's Guidance Through Scripture

*At the end of each chapter that describes one of God's four guid-
ance systems is a page, much like this one, to help you apply the
system to a specific decision in your life. Appendix C also contains a complete set of these pages, which you may copy for other
decisions, as well as a sample summary page to aid you in integrating the information you gain from all of the systems.*

For this situation, for this decision, or for today, the Bible, augmented by other Christian wisdom, seems to be providing me
with guidance in the following ways:

General Insights: Is this matter disputable or nondisputable?
What moral principles or ideas seem to apply?

Verse or passage reference   Relevant message for me right now

Bible stories or characters: Is my situation similar to any
stories of the Bible? What can I learn from the examples of the
people in the Bible?

Specific leadings as I read and study Scripture: In my regular study, have any verses "spoken" to me, or have certain verses come to mind that seem to have special meaning in my situation?

Verse or passage reference   Relevant message for me right now

Do others agree with my interpretation? Remember, God's guidance is a light for our journey, not a full map.

Guidance System #2

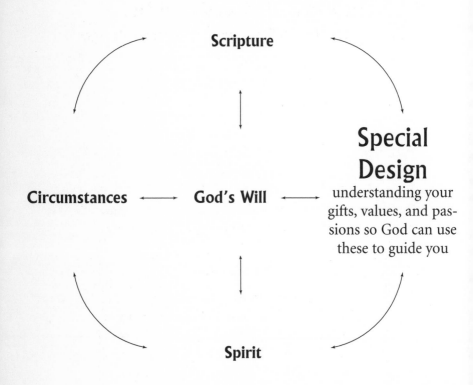

Scripture

Special Design
understanding your gifts, values, and passions so God can use these to guide you

Circumstances **God's Will**

Spirit

Chapter 3

How Has God Designed Us?
Finding Guidance Through Our Special Design

Even the stork in the sky
knows her appointed seasons,
and the dove, the swift and the thrush
observe the time of their migration.
But my people do not know the
requirements of the Lord.

—Jeremiah 8:7

Before you read this chapter, think about:

1. How would you rank your comfort with finding God's guidance through your special design? Use a scale of 1 ("I'm not sure if this works") to 10 ("I'm very comfortable with this form of God's guidance").

2. How do you think this piece of God's system for finding God's will works best? What questions do you have about it?

3. What are your biggest worries or fears about using how you are designed to find God's guidance for your life?

Here in Minnesota it's easy to wonder about birds. They seem to know the time of their migration, but if we're still seeing robins as we tune up the snowblowers, we want to shoo them south. Yet robins, much as we worry, recognize the season. They always manage to leave town before the inevitable Thanksgiving blizzard, letting cardinals and blue jays and chickadees keep us company during the winter months.

Mallard ducks are supposed to vacate this state with the robins for the winter, but sometimes they get fooled. Not far from us is a pond that stays open year-round. Paddling in water heated by the generators of a nearby condominium complex, a few hundred ducks stay there all winter, huddling close together when subzero blasts freeze the edges of their little refuge.

Other birds are able to weather Minnesota's cold. But when mallards act outside of the laws of nature and remain here for the hostile winter months, they lose their freedom. It's too cold for them to fly.

When you act outside of how God designed you—and the atmospheres where you flourish—you're stuck huddled in some forsaken spot, out of your element and out of energy. Like robins and mallards, humans are designed for certain places and atmospheres. But when you heed your special design—the second system for discovering God's will—you gain freedom to fly.

Our book *LifeKeys: Discovering Who You Are, Why You're Here, What You Do Best*[1] was written to help people understand their unique, God-given design. The following chart shows the role each of the five *LifeKeys* plays in helping you discover your design and then, as explained in this chapter, how God might use elements of your design to guide you.

---

[1] Jane A.G. Kise, David Stark, and Sandra Krebs Hirsh, *LifeKeys: Discovering Who You Are, Why You're Here, What You Do Best* (Minneapolis: Bethany House Publishers, 1996). See also Kevin Johnson and Jane Kise, *Find Your Fit* (Minneapolis: Bethany House Publishers, 1998).

Your LifeKeys	How this helps you understand your design	How God might use these to guide you
Life Gifts (natural talents) Spiritual Gifts	Life gifts and spiritual gifts tell you what you do best.	By giving you specific gifts, God has already shown you the kinds of activities or work for which you are needed in God's plans.
Values Passions	Values and passions help you to recognize the purposes or causes on which you could act with enthusiasm or joy.	By influencing your values and passions, God can guide you toward the purposes to which you are called in service to God and to humankind.
Personality Type	Personality type—often in partnership with values—helps you discern the places, settings, or atmospheres that will appeal to you the most.	By honoring your personality, God can communicate with you in ways that you best understand.

Are We All Really Gifted?

When my first child was born, a friend wrote a note to the baby asking, "How was the trip from the mind of God?" I was already overwhelmed by the sight of this tiny, new life, but the letter crystallized for me the huge role God plays in designing each one of us.

—David

Each of us was designed by the Creator of the universe:

For you created my inmost being;
  you knit me together in my mother's womb.
I praise you because I am fearfully
  and wonderfully made;
  your works are wonderful,
  I know that full well.

My frame was not hidden from you
   when I was made in the secret place.
—Psalm 139:13-15

Not only did God design you, but that design included specific gifts and talents. If Peter writes to us, "Like good stewards of the manifold grace of God, serve one another with whatever gift *each of you* has received" (1 Peter 4:10 NRSV, emphasis added), then we each must have a gift.

But there's a problem in looking to how God made us for guidance: Most people have never taken the time to discover how they were designed. Our book *LifeKeys* grew from classes we taught to assist people with this process. We see three major reasons why people have a hard time tapping into the guidance system of how they're designed.

They don't feel worthy of being gifted by God in any way. Perhaps they were raised by parents who considered children a curse instead of a blessing. Or they've suffered so many employment setbacks that they've lost confidence in their usefulness. Or their church or workplace pigeonholes people and doesn't let them serve in new ways.

They don't know themselves. As one *LifeKeys* participant said, "Where were you when I was nineteen?" Many of us choose a life path based on the expectations of others, an inheritance of a business or position, or practical considerations. Sometimes these methods line up with God's plans for us; other times they keep God from showing us how we are designed. And once we choose a career path, there's often little time to reflect about the good works we may be specifically equipped to accomplish. There's little opportunity to ask, "What is my role in God's kingdom? What purposes will be left undone if I ignore how I am designed?"

They're not satisfied with what God has given them. When we taught our first class in helping people find their giftedness, we were struck by how difficult self-acceptance is for people.

Even within our congregation of professionals, two-thirds of our participants didn't like what they discovered about themselves. Some, especially if they made the mistake of comparing their gifts with those of others, were convinced that they were absent the day God handed out gifts. Others didn't believe that their gifts were important enough that they could do anything significant for God.

> *At a New Year's party, several women and I were discussing the resolutions we had made. Almost all of those present had resolved to be more like some other woman they named. This seemed so sad to me after what I had learned through* LifeKeys *not too long before. I told them, "I don't want to be like anyone else. I want to be more like who I was designed to be."*
>
> —Bethany, 42, homemaker

It's one thing to know how you are gifted; it's another thing to like what you discover. And that's our goal: to help you appreciate the way God created you until your desire is to be more and more like yourself. Before God can guide you through how you're designed, you have to trust that God chose what is best for you. Otherwise—at some level—you're saying that you could do a better job than God did in designing you. Consider this: People who suffer from low self-esteem have a lot in common with people who think of no one but themselves. Both views are still centered on the self.

Although it sounds contradictory, exploring how God has gifted you is actually the way to stop concentrating on yourself. Let's see why.

Is It Selfish to Look at Your Design?

You might wonder if exploring who you are could block you from concentrating on God. One school of thought holds that our focus should be God, not our design, to determine what God wants us to do. They might say, "Doesn't God gift us after we step forward to serve? Aren't we really just looking for the easy way if we only want to do what we do well? And won't we then depend on our own abilities rather than lean on God?"

We have a different perspective on this issue:

First, the Bible tells us to use the gifts we have, which implies that we know what they are:

> God has given each of us the ability to do certain things well. So if God has given you the ability to prophesy, speak out when you have faith that God is speaking through you. If your gift is that of serving others, serve them well. If you are a teacher, do a good job of teaching. If your gift is to encourage others, do it! If you have money, share it generously. If God has given you leadership ability, take the responsibility seriously. And if you have a gift for showing kindness to others, do it gladly. (Romans 12:6-8 NLT)

Second, as we observe and enjoy all that God has created, we see evidence that God takes great joy in the unique design of each living thing, giving animals the proficiencies they need not only to survive but to thrive in their own environments. The eagle's eyesight allows it to spot the movement of a mouse far below on the ground. Ducks have webbed feet, while ostriches don't. If God knew us before we were born, wouldn't our design include just what we need? And if we've all been given gifts and talents, wouldn't God want us to use them?

While we firmly believe that God wants us to understand how we are fearfully and wonderfully made, we also acknowledge that there is a danger in encouraging people to work within their gifts. Sometimes, even in the face of a disaster, Christians decide they don't have to step forward to serve. They ignore the other guidance systems and excuse themselves by saying, "That isn't my gift."

In a perfect world, that might be okay. If everyone accepted with joy the way he or she was created, there would be no lack of servants. None of us would have to serve outside our gifts. If God wanted something done, people with the right mix of gifts and calling would step forward. But within the imperfect reality of the church are countless people who don't understand their purpose. God has provided the workers; they simply don't recognize their gifts and calling.

Within these circumstances, then, sometimes we have to boldly meet needs that may not play to our gifting. As the children's ministry director at our church points out, "When I get down to filling the last twenty of the 250 slots for Sunday school teachers, I stop worrying about whether a potential volunteer has the gift of teaching. My only requirement is a detectable pulse! I'll find some way to help them develop the skills they need."

Unfortunately, many times a lack of volunteers reflects the way people put some gifts on pedestals while downplaying the importance of others. People forget that it isn't the gift they are using, but the power of the God who gave them that gift that matters to the work of the church. Read closely the words of the first apostles as they struggled with how to do everything in the early church:

> So the Twelve gathered all the disciples together and said, "It would not be right for us to neglect the ministry of the word of God in order to wait on tables. Brothers, choose seven men from among you who are known to be full of the Spirit and wisdom. We will turn this responsibility over to them and will give our attention to prayer and the ministry of the word" (Acts 6:2-4).

This decision allowed the apostles to concentrate on what they did well. They weren't looking to get out of other tasks; they understood at a deep level that the way to further God's kingdom is for each person to do his or her own part.

The third reason for looking at our design is that identifying what we do well also shows us what we don't do well. This not only highlights our need for God, but the interdependency of God's people. God created us to be dependent on one another, so chances are we won't have all of the gifts and talents a task calls for. Moses needed his brother Aaron to speak before Pharaoh. He needed the help of his father-in-law to organize and settle disputes for the Israelites. And more than anything else, Moses needed God's help. Understanding our giftedness is actually an avenue for acknowledging how little we can do by ourselves.

Whenever we (Jane and David) write or teach together, we're amazed at how much more God can do through the two of us than through either of us alone. David's formal seminary training and pastoral experience coupled with Jane's business background and years of independent study bring insights and teaching methods both broader and deeper than either method of schooling would alone. David's instincts for outlining and connecting the major points we want to make complements Jane's ability to find the right stories and structure our content. Ecclesiastes makes clear, "Though one may be overpowered, two can defend themselves. A cord of three strands is not quickly broken" (Ecclesiastes 4:12). With God as the third strand in our writing, we have resources and gifts far beyond what either of us can do alone. And we're acutely aware of how much of the credit God deserves.

You can partner with other people or find ways to subdivide the work. Habitat for Humanity, the organization that pairs the services of volunteers with people who need assistance in building a home, is a great example. If you can't wield a hammer, maybe you can bring a meal, deliver supplies, or coordinate volunteer schedules. They make it hard to say, "But I don't do windows or staple shingles." When we see God at work, we can look more deeply at all of the jobs involved and perhaps discover we fit after all.

Finally, we don't believe that God is so heartless that we would receive gifts we weren't meant to use. Would a human coach ever pour time and effort into helping a child become a great runner or swimmer and then say, "No more racing. It's the basketball court or nothing!" No, we try to help our children find what they do well. Why would we expect anything from God other than a desire to bring us to the places where we can flourish?

According to *Webster's*, to *flourish* means "to be in a state of activity or production, to reach a height of development or influence, to thrive." People who are flourishing are capable of being incredibly effective kingdom workers, convinced that they are carrying out God's will to the best of their abilities.

Rejoicing in What We Were Given

Those abilities—the things that we do well and that bring us joy or fulfillment—are our life gifts and spiritual gifts. Life gifts are given to all of us so we can make a living, build relationships, and function as humans. In contrast, spiritual gifts are given so we can carry out God's purposes. The fact that we are meant to find fulfillment in using these gifts is a radical concept to many of the people we've taught.

> *In my mind, Christian service was a duty, something you had to do, the religious equivalent of taking out the trash. So I volunteered for tasks with the same attitude I had when emptying wastebaskets—someone had to do it, and I at least would be conscientious enough to do it right. Tallying up stewardship pledges, ironing 100 vests for the children's choir, scheduling ushers…whatever the task, I gritted my teeth until it was over.*
>
> *I think I used to volunteer for the things I enjoyed least just so I'd feel I'd done my duty. Now that I know my gifts, I'm excited by the difference between duty and fulfillment. While I know that even the most fitting tasks will bring some frustrations—after all, even on vacation, fun is interrupted by lost suitcases or rained-out picnics—I also know that I'm at my best for God when I'm doing what I do best.*
>
> —Steve, 52, accountant

You'd find it silly if a pelican decided to dig for earthworms or if a mallard duck decided to walk from Minnesota to Florida. We are meant to do what we are created to do—it's the path to the joy Jesus promises us. God guarantees that these gifts are just right for us:

> Is there anyone among you who, if your child asks for bread, will give a stone? Or if the child asks for a fish, will give a snake? If you then, who are evil, know how to give good gifts to your children, how much more will your Father in heaven give good things to those who ask him! (Matthew 7:9-11 NRSV)

However, if your gifts aren't the ones that our culture celebrates—if you aren't a star athlete or musician or leader—you may not realize how gifted you are. You may even think that everyone knows how to fix things or organize things or lend a listening ear. Appendix A contains a list of both life gifts and spiritual gifts. If you haven't completed *LifeKeys,* this appendix can introduce you to the topic, but most people will need to dig deeper to understand their giftedness.

If you assume that God shortchanged you when gifts were handed out—and that's what you're saying if you don't like the gifts you have—then we want you to hear three things.

1. You are not alone. In the book of 1 Corinthians, Paul wrote to people two thousand years ago who struggled with the same issues.

> Yes, there are many parts, but only one body. The eye can never say to the hand, "I don't need you." The head can't say to the feet, "I don't need you." In fact, some of the parts that seem weakest and least important are really the most necessary. And the parts we regard as less honorable are those we clothe with the greatest care. So we carefully protect from the eyes of others those parts that should not be seen, while other parts do not require this special care. So God has put the body together in such a way that extra honor and care are given to those parts that have less dignity. This makes for harmony among the members, so that all the members care for each other equally. If one part suffers, all the parts suffer with it, and if one part is honored, all the parts are glad. Now all of you together are Christ's body, and each one of you is a separate and necessary part of it. (1 Corinthians 12:20-27 NLT)

2. You don't appreciate what God can do through your gifts. Lives have been changed by the gift of a simple visit, a note of encouragement, or consistent intercessory prayer. Remember, God's power isn't dependent on what you can do but on who God is. The question isn't whether you're glad you got a particular gift but whether the body of Christ needs it. Your gifts are for others, not for you. When you use your gifts, the worth of what you do isn't measured by whether you feel you've accomplished anything. Its value is in whether someone else is served, whether God is honored, whether the kingdom of God is lived here on earth. Your small job may be essential to God's purposes.

3. God cannot guide you through your design until you accept who you are. Again, much of finding God's will depends on your willingness to do whatever it is you discover God wants you to do. If you're one of the many who deep down says, "But I don't like my gifts," keep in mind that back in Acts 6 when the apostles were asking others to wait on tables, preaching and praying weren't cushy jobs! They didn't bring praise or glamour. Paul describes the life of the apostles like this:

> For it seems to me that God has put us apostles on display at the end of the procession, like men condemned to die in the arena. We have been made a spectacle to the whole universe, to angels as well as to men. We are fools for Christ, but you are so wise in Christ! We are weak, but you are strong! You are honored, we are dishonored! To this very hour we go hungry and thirsty, we are in rags, we are brutally treated, we are homeless. We work hard with our own hands. When we are cursed, we bless; when we are persecuted, we endure it; when we are slandered, we answer kindly. Up to this moment we have become the scum of the earth, the refuse of the world. (1 Corinthians 4:9-11)

Paul, Peter, and James didn't ask to be admired just because they had spiritual gifts that put them at the center of attention. Somehow over the centuries we've lost the message that all gifts and talents are equal in the eyes of God.

Applying What You Do Well

When you know your life gifts and spiritual gifts, you know *what* God might ask you to do. You know whether you're going to persuade others, manage time or resources, teach, use artistic skills, solve problems—whatever those talents are. There is much more to be done to discover *where* and *why* you'll put those gifts to work. Knowing what you do best, though, is a huge part of the equation for two of the most complex types of decisions we make: our vocation and how we're going to serve God.

Using your gifts to guide you isn't being selfish. Yes, you can use your gifts for selfish motives. You can lead others so that you make money rather than so that they see God. You can employ artistic skills to celebrate God's creation or to make a blockbuster movie (or even do both!).

However, God can work wonders when we decide to put our gifts to work for the Body of Christ. Jeff[2], for example, grew up with the toughest of family backgrounds in a tough part of New York City. He definitely had talents for risk-taking, organization, and persuasion, but he used them as a drug smuggler. By the time Jeff was twenty-one, he owned condos in New York and Malibu. He claims that most of the national government of Bolivia would have mobilized on his behalf because of their economic gains from his drug trafficking. That prominence, though, caused U.S. forces to target him, and he was eventually caught and thrown in prison. A New York judge put him in solitary confinement, where Jeff took a good look at his life and became a Christian.

Jeff later thanked the judge for forcing him into a situation where he had to face who he was. Five years after his release, the former drug runner was using those same gifts for risk-taking, organization, and persuasion to lead a major evangelistic crusade and mission to Ireland. That's the power of combining knowing God and knowing your gifts.

Following God's guidance isn't always the easy path, and it is only natural that we might balk at times or question our motives when the way seems natural. The mere fact that you are worried about whether or not you are selfish is half the battle. Even if you have these doubts about serving through your gifts, understand that *God cannot guide you through how you have been gifted until you believe:*

---

2 His name has been changed.

God loves you.
At your very core is the image of God.
Inside your soul is a dwelling fit for God.
The gifts you have were chosen to fit with how God
designed you.
The gifts you have are exactly those God needs you to have.
Using your gifts is the path to fulfillment.

LifeKeys begins from the premise of Ephesians 2:10: "For we are God's workmanship, created in Christ Jesus to do good works, which God prepared in advance for us to do." God can guide us to finding those good works by helping us discover who we are, why we're here, and what we do best.

Being Guided by the Uniqueness of You

Jane doesn't get asked to repair cars or sing in the choir, but to teach and write. David doesn't get asked to prepare tax returns or design new sanctuaries, but to motivate others and help them understand God in new ways. Understanding what you do well narrows down what you might do for God. However, that doesn't mean that you need to say yes to every opportunity that comes your way to use your gifts. Considering a few basic principles can help you narrow down how God wants you to use them.

1. Analyze your choices. When you are asked to do something, list out which life gifts and spiritual gifts you will actually use. Is it a good fit for you right now? Can you say yes to one part of the job and no to another? Chart out the options. One of our friends wanted to help with Vacation Bible School, but since she couldn't be present every morning she said no when asked to lead a preschool class. While that role fit within her gifts of teaching and mercy, she decided to look for opportunities to use her gift of helps instead. When she asked what else she might do, she learned she could prepare all of the treats for the preschool and deliver them early in the day. She was able to help with the preschoolers, yet leave herself free to meet other commitments.

2. Analyze your time. Look at each of your options by asking, "How much of my time will I spend operating within my life gifts or spiritual gifts?" Some experts recommend that it be at least 60 percent of your time if you are to remain energized. However, there are two exceptions:

- Most people are out of balance during certain seasons of life, be it while child-rearing, recovering from illness, or other temporary circumstances.
- It's harder to find jobs that utilize certain life gifts and spiritual gifts. Artists may have to settle for using their talents on the weekend. People with the gift of discernment may not use it very often, but it may still be a key part of what they do.

3. Determine what gifts you lack to get the job done. This doesn't mean a door is slammed shut: Jesus sent the apostles out two by two. Jane's husband, Brian, for example, is a great leader for games and outings, but he hesitated taking over as head of their son's Cub Scout pack because of all of the administrative and organizational work involved. Those tasks are within Jane's gifts, so between the two of them, they can handle being Cubmaster.

4. Imagine what will happen if you say no. Weigh your passion level against your sense of duty before you say yes or no. In his book *Guilt and Grace*[3], Paul Tournier observes, "False guilt comes from saying no to people…. The only true guilt comes from saying no to God."

Sometimes people tell us, "But if I don't continue this responsibility, the activity [committee, event, ministry, etc.] won't take place." And we answer, "That may be. But if it is really important to other people, they will come forward to take over and you can move on to something that will energize you instead of drain you." This is *true*. Letting go of something may allow it to be reborn in a way that will attract new help or leadership. And perhaps God wants you to move on to something different.

---

3 Paul Tournier, *Guilt and Grace* (New York: Harper & Row, 1962).

If you are ready to move on, you might still use the same life gifts and spiritual gifts, but the purposes for which you use them may change. To show you those purposes, God often acts to influence your values or passions, two other facets of who you are.

Finding Guidance Through Our Values

Values are those things that feel important to you, define your character, supply meaning to work and life, and compel you to take a stand. Different life stages emphasize different values, and God can influence us through the ordering of our values. Our values, like passions, rise and fall in importance for us. If you doubt this, just picture how the value of financial security changes when you're handed a pink slip. Or how traditions shift in importance after marriage or the birth of children or the death of a parent. Think of it this way: God *gives* us our life gifts, spiritual gifts, and, as we will see in a moment, personality types. These don't change, although we may use different ones during different seasons of our lives. However, God wants to *influence* our values and passions. These *do* change, and the changes are important clues to where God wants us to go next.

As part of *LifeKeys,* people sort through fifty-one values, choosing just eight that are most important to them.

> *I attended* LifeKeys *because I was dissatisfied with my job in the marketing department of a large corporation. There weren't enough promotion opportunities and I felt that my creativity wasn't honored: I spent most of my time working on other people's ideas. When I finished sorting my values cards, I recorded my top eight values—and left the room! In putting achievement, advancement, creativity, and so on as my most important values, I saw that I had sorted my family out of what I value most. I spent over an hour thinking through what I really valued. Getting promoted isn't as important right now as time with my four kids. This more laid-back job is just what I need for the next five to ten years. I'll still have the chance to find a more challenging, fulfilling position.*
>
> —Rick, 37, marketing executive

God guided Rick by helping him see that he was focusing on the wrong values for this season of his life. Satisfaction and fulfillment came by changing his view of what was important to him.

We've seen God guide people in many other ways through their values:

- Karen knew that her people skills were better than the administrative skills her job called for, but when she made a few mistakes, she thought she wasn't being diligent enough. After perceiving that her top value was serving others, Karen understood her struggle. Her current job didn't let her help people directly and she therefore sometimes found it hard to concentrate. Although she couldn't change jobs right away, Karen developed some new procedures to catch her own mistakes and took a volunteer counseling position that fulfilled her values.

- Noah and Krystall, newly married, compared values to help them make decisions about leisure time and how they might serve God both separately and together.

- When Jeremy realized how severely a top-down decision had violated his value for cooperation, he knew that God was asking him to confront his boss about how things had been handled. While the meeting wasn't pleasant, he persuaded his boss to pull back from his position and gather more input from others who were involved.

- Terri ranked her values and used that information to prioritize her commitments and schedule her time. She used them as a foundation for writing a mission statement.

- Phil looked at his values and finally realized that he had good reason to leave his stable, well-paying job: His values for peace and the nurturing of human life clashed with his company's dependence on the defense industry.

For God to guide you in this way, you have to know what your values are. While we think using the values cards in the back of *LifeKeys* is one of the most engaging ways to define your values, you can also sit down with pencil and paper. Think through things that are important to you, what you base decisions on, or what causes you to take a stand. What do you value?

And once you know, take a moment to listen to God about what you've put down. Do any of your values conflict with what you're doing now? Are they in conflict with the people with whom you live or work? And are they the values God wants you to hold in this season of your life? Do any of the others tug at you? God may be trying to guide you through what these values are saying to you, perhaps drawing your attention toward a new passion upon which you might act for God.

What Has God Put in Your Heart?

Passions are the last *LifeKey* we ask people to explore—God uses them to guide us to the places our gifts are most needed.

> *I was asked to write a script for a children's event at church. While I had the skills and talents to do so and had helped with similar things in the past, I didn't feel passionate about it. Rather than just say no, I suggested several other people whom I knew were trying to gain experience as writers. One of them was thrilled to be asked, the job was completed, and I managed to stick to the projects I believed God wanted me to focus on.*
>
> —Jane

Some of the changes in our passions happen naturally. Maybe your own children are past the toddler stage and the thought of changing diapers in the church nursery has lost its appeal— or perhaps you miss your own babies and happily volunteer to rock the little ones at church each Sunday.

> *I was torn between continuing as a hands-on youth minister and taking a more administrative role with a national youth organization. During the time my wife and I were mulling over the choices, I took my own children to a local amusement park. After three trips on the mega roller coaster with my ten-year-old, I decided I no longer had at least one part of what it takes to be a youth pastor—handling rides without getting sick!*
>
> —Jordan, 34, pastor

Changes in passions may be harder to detect if you choose them through a sense of duty. Perhaps you've been on the board of a certain ministry for so long that you feel you have to be there. Or everyone assumes that you'll continue as head cook for the big pancake breakfast, just as you have for the past five years. Or that you'll take the meeting minutes because you're so good at it. Maybe you will, but maybe it's time to consider whether these commitments are keeping you from moving to a new calling.

Start with a few basic questions about your passions to see if you are allowing God to influence their course. Are you getting to use the gifts you are most drawn to? Which of your activities would you be willing to continue if you knew someone else would take over? What long-term goals do you have? Are your short-term passions moving you toward those goals or away from them? Are you saying no to some things you'd really like to help with because you've said yes to other things?

Passions need to be tested to ensure they come from God and not from our own desires. As you face decisions, ask yourself:

- Would Scripture prohibit me from acting on this passion?
- Do those who understand my gifts and talents believe I would be effective exercising this passion?
- Do the trusted people around me see this passion as a possibility grounded in reality (allowing for the reality that we can partner with others or that God may help us stretch beyond our normal abilities for a specific cause)?
- How well do I understand my motives? Could they possibly be too self-serving?
- As I pursue this passion, does my motivation increase or decrease the more I work with it? Am I being overwhelmed by difficulties or is it truly not my passion?[4]

Doing God's will isn't about gritting your teeth and getting through the day, although you will have periods of frustration no matter how passionate you are about your tasks in the body of Christ. But, in conjunction with the other guidance systems, you can trust that God is calling you to the tasks that

---

4 *LifeKeys*, 194.

you care most about and that fit best with how you were
created.

Being Guided Through What We Do and Understand Best

Our gifts, values, and passions are ways God guides us through
our unique, God-given design. But God also guides us through
our uniqueness by "speaking" to us as we are. Take a look at how
differently God approaches people; the Bible doesn't give a standard method for convincing people to follow God's instructions.
While there are many examples of this, we'll explore how God
honors each personality type and how God often speaks to us
in ways that our special gifts allow us to comprehend.

The theory of psychological type was made popular through
the Myers-Briggs Type Indicator® (MBTI)[5]. Type theory puts
forth the idea that we have natural preferences for how we like
to:

Take in energy

Extraverts (E) gain energy through activity and interaction
with others.

Introverts (I) gain energy through spending time in their inner
world of thoughts and ideas.

Gather information

Sensors (S) rely on their five senses for information.

Intuitives (N) gather information through insights, inferences,
and connections.

Make decisions

Thinkers (T) rely on objectivity, logic, cause/effect or other
systematic models for making decisions.

Feelers (F) subjectively place themselves into a situation, "walking in the other person's shoes" to make decisions.

---

[5] If the 4-letter codes of the MBTI are Greek to you, we suggest reading chapter 4 of
LifeKeys, or *LifeTypes* by Sandra Krebs Hirsh and Jean Kummerow (Warner Books, 1989).
The MBTI is the most widely used personality assessment in the United States and helps
explain normal differences among people.

Approach life

Judgers (J) want to plan their work and work their plan.

Perceivers (P) want to be flexible, ready to take advantage of the best each moment has to offer.

These eight preferences combine to describe sixteen different psychological types. These are not boxes into which we place people, but tools we can use to understand what we and others do naturally and how we might best communicate with each other.

God speaks to different personality types in ways they best understand. Those sixteen psychological types are often divided into four fundamental ways we function: Sensing, Intuition, Thinking, and Feeling.

Sensors (ISTJ, ISFJ, ESTP, ESFP) believe what they experience through their five senses. They may be more drawn to the practical applications of faith than its mysteries. The blind man whom Jesus healed may have echoed the sentiments of many Sensing types when he told the Pharisees, "Whether [Jesus] is a sinner or not, I don't know. One thing I do know. I was blind but now I see!" (John 9:25). He didn't need any other proof or explanation. Thomas had the opportunity to put his hand into the wound in Jesus' side—Jesus honored the doubts only his senses could answer. Many of the parables use what people can touch or see to help them understand God: a mustard seed, lost sheep, birds of the air, and lilies of the field.

Sensors may be most comfortable trusting guidance that is confirmed by their senses. They may see God's hand in the actions of another or see affirmation in what has worked or held true in the past.

Intuitives (INFJ, INTJ, ENFP, ENTP) are more open to hearing God through dreams, flashes of intuition, or by making connections between the seen and the unseen. Daniel knew that he correctly understood the king's dreams. Peter seems to have been guided this way as we hear him declare, "You are the Christ, the Son of the living God" (Matthew 16:16).

Peter also trusted the dream he had about clean and unclean foods before meeting Cornelius. (See Acts 10.) Intuitives don't always have to have all the facts laid out before they are willing to make a decision or choice. If you aren't an Intuitive, you may think they're working on instinct with no solid foundation, but Intuitives *know* when they can trust their interpretation of a situation.

Intuitives may be most comfortable trusting guidance they receive through these flashes of intuition. One Intuitive told us that when he was sixteen, he heard other boys ridiculing priests and the tough vows they took. Right then and there, he *knew* he was meant to be a priest; in thirty years he hasn't regretted his choice.

Thinkers (ISTP, INTP, ESTJ, ENTJ) seek clear understanding of what is true. Jesus spent time with Nicodemus in pure intellectual discussion. Paul made use of clear, logical arguments in his letters to establish policies for the fledgling church. Thinkers often have to define something for themselves before they can form a position or believe in it.

As Jane interviewed people for her book *SoulTypes*[6], several Thinkers told her that they had to define God's love in terms of how other people acted out of love, the behaviors they displayed, and the results that followed, before they understood what it meant to be loved by God. They were then able to objectively shift their behavior to show responses others considered loving. Logic and cause/effect reasoning brought them to a place of grace that no amount of emotion or personal involvement could.

In decision-making, Thinkers might trust most the guidance God provides through their reasoning when they see the clear logic of a path balanced against the input of the other guidance systems. C. S. Lewis, for example, applied logic to the question of who Christ is. In *Mere Christianity*, he argued that you must either accept Christ's claims to be the Son of God or declare

---

6 Jane Kise, *SoulTypes: Finding the Spiritual Path That Is Right for You.* (New York: Hyperion Books, 1998).

him a madman. The evidence logically contradicts the suggestion that Jesus was merely a great teacher. "A man who was merely a man and said the sort of things Jesus said would not be a great moral teacher. He would either be a lunatic—on a level with the man who says he is a poached egg—or else he would be the Devil of Hell."[7] Lewis's logic has helped many others in their search for the truth about Christianity.

Feelers (ISFP, INFP, ESFJ, ENFJ) are influenced by relationships and seeing how matters affect them personally. Jesus took the time to dine with Zacchaeus. He personalized his message to the woman at the well. He discerned how each person could be reached most effectively.

Feelers may trust the information God gives them through relationships, through symbols teeming with personal meaning, or even through the words of a song or poem that speak directly to their situation. Feelers recognize when their hearts have been warmed, whether or not facts or logic are present, and can trust what their emotions are telling them to do if they check this guidance against the other guidance systems.

Thus, while a Feeler might want to check through such details as salary considerations or job responsibilities, he or she might decide between two positions based on how friendly the potential co-workers seem and consider that relational input part of God's guidance for them. A Thinker may start with the pros and cons of each choice. Intuitives might imagine themselves in each place. Which might be more comfortable? Sensors might list the facts they have and choose based on what they know for sure. All four types, though, would need to check what they have learned through their dominant function against:
  • the wisdom of the Bible;
  • which life gifts and spiritual gifts are needed;
  • input from the Holy Spirit (chapter 4);
  • input from circumstances (chapter 5).

---

7 C. S. Lewis, *Mere Christianity* (New York: Macmillan Publishing Company, 1960), 56.

The more you understand about your psychological type, the more you can use it to determine whether you are making a wise decision. Answers that come through your dominant function are often more trustworthy than those that come through the other functions.

My husband and I were trying to decide whether to add a third child to our family. Being a Feeling type, my heart was telling me that I needed to be a mother one more time. I missed coloring at the kitchen table with a small child. I felt my two sons would benefit from helping nurture a tiny brother or sister. I also paid attention to the pangs I felt when I saw other mothers with babies. I thought, I'm not ready to say good-bye to those experiences. *My husband, a Thinker, still wavered. He even joked about it one evening when he found me doting over my eldest's baby book. I cried myself to sleep that night, wondering what it would take to make us jointly ready for a new baby.*

The next morning he called me from work. "Honey, I've determined that we can have another child—I've got it all worked out on the spreadsheet in front of me. I've added up our different sources of income and calculated the results if I take my sabbatical year to coincide with the end of your maternity leave. With the savings on day care and the fact that our current home is big enough, we'll be fine."

About ten months later, our little girl was born.

—Judie, 35, pastor

Using How You Were Created to Discover God's Guidance

Finally, God often gives us messages through the gifts we know best how to use. When you are facing major decisions, put those gifts to work! David and Jane both have life gifts for research and synthesizing—major decisions send us to stacks of books, conversations with experts, and other forms of investigation. Both of us find that when we pull from a myriad of resources, then check what we learn with the other forms of guidance, we often discover what God wants us to do.

However, neither of us has a clear gift for discernment. As Intuitive Feelers, we're too inclined to believe the best of everyone and everything. We therefore often get second opinions about business decisions from people who have this gift.

Maybe you are the opposite of us. You seem to "know," to be able to discern what is of God and what is not of God, but you find it helpful when others gather the information to back what you have discerned.

Or maybe your overwhelming gift is faith. You trust your decisions when you have that unmistakable conviction that God wants to have something done.

Look at your life gifts and spiritual gifts. How might you use them in the decision-making process? In what ways does God use them to speak to you?

Know Thyself, and Then?

Of course, this means that each and every one of us is individually guided by God. It doesn't matter whether you've had visions or heard voices—God has already spoken to you through how you were created. Yes, there is more to learn and discern, but you can't say that "individual guidance only happens to people who are more spiritual (or more nutty) than I am." All of us were designed with a purpose in mind; the question is whether we choose to pay attention to our uniqueness.

Knowing yourself is of utmost importance for choosing a career, for making decisions, for building relationships, for enjoying life. But all of that is of secondary importance to God. Yes, God wants each of us to make our lives count through these things, but more important, God wants us to invest our gifts and talents and values—all of what we have been given—in the work God needs to have done in this world.

God doesn't ask us to worry about the level of gifts and talents we have, although we can work to improve how well we use them. What is important to God is whether we believe we are gifted *and whether we believe God is acting through us and with us.*

What if birds consciously set out to fly? If they had to deliberately analyze the wind and air currents? Send the correct impulses to each muscle and tendon to move their wings? Determine where to go? They'd be so busy trying to process multiple inputs and directions that they'd never go more than a few yards from the nest. But they don't worry. They simply fly. They know their bodies can do it.

If you believe God can do it, you can trust your gifts and talents in the same way. Get moving, start flapping, see who can come along with you, and find out what you can do in partnership with God.

> *Have you given me all the pieces?*
> *Can I really solve the puzzle of my life?*
> *If this is what I do well, what am I to do for you?*
> *Shouldn't I know where I'm going?*
> *Yet,*
> *if I really knew, would I be discouraged?*
> *Not happy or satisfied enough to work at what I am*
> *doing now?*
> *Or would I be puffed up with pride,*
> *slowing my efforts or relying on myself instead of on*
> *you?*
> *I'll wait, God.*
> *You placed the pieces within me.*
> *I'll let you help me assemble them*
> *bit by bit...*
> *as I'm ready. Amen.*

Tips for Using Your Special Design

Your psychological type gives you insight as to how you make decisions, as well as input for those decisions. Each psychological preference has inherent strengths as well as possible pitfalls for this process. Take a moment to read through the following chart. For your preferences, highlight which of the following are true for you.

Strengths	Weaknesses
Sensors	
Accurately assessing reality	Wanting certainty on all the facts of every scenario
Gaining wisdom from past experiences	
Evaluating alternatives based on measurable evidence	Dismissing alternatives for which they have no relative past experience
	Being closed off to generating more speculative alternatives
Intuitives	
Listing possibilities, alternatives, or explanations	Not acknowledging the restraints or facts of a situation
Being willing to act on a hunch or their personal insights	Denying reality, not listening to advice that might contradict their hunches
Thinking outside the box, trying new things, exploring new territory	Ignoring tried and true traditions or methods that might be the best
Thinkers	
Relying on measurable and therefore objective criteria: cost, time frames, etc.	Ignoring how alternatives might impact others or themselves personally
Using logical thinking to analyze alternatives	Ignoring other rational processes such as determining values or assessing personal meaning

Strengths	Weaknesses
Thinkers (continued)	
Developing models or other decision-making criteria	Forgetting that not everything conforms to a model when people are involved
Feelers	
Evaluating how each person will be affected	Overlooking the importance of guidelines or standards
Acknowledging the impact of their own likes and dislikes on alternatives	Not giving enough weight to objectivity, facts, or logical outcomes
Using values as a central criteria	Forgetting other important criteria such as money, time commitments, etc.

In addition:

- While Extraverts often process decisions best when they can talk them through with other people, they need time alone to research and reflect.
- While Introverts may prefer privacy for life decisions, they need input from others to generate additional alternatives and factors they hadn't considered.

And be forewarned:

- While Judgers may benefit from their orderly approach to decision-making, with its timelines, steps, and goals, they may reach conclusions too quickly, before they've really had time to explore all the possibilities adequately.
- While Perceivers may benefit from their ability to be open-minded about the process and the optimal point of resolution, they may evaluate and procrastinate for so long that some of their alternatives actually disappear.

If you know your psychological type, look at pages 75–79 to determine your dominant function and how it might help with decisions. Does the description ring true to you? Looking back through what you've highlighted in the above chart, what do you need to keep in mind about your psychological type, both positive and negative, as you seek God's guidance?

Reflections for Your Own LifeDirections

1. Look through our main points in this chapter. Which one caught your attention the most? Why?
   - God created you uniquely; that design is part of how God guides you.
   - God can't guide you through this system until you like who you are.
   - Because this is one of the guidance systems, all of us experience individual guidance.
   - God guides you: through the gifts you've been given; by influencing your values and passions.
   - You can use your strengths and gifts in making decisions.

2. Reflecting on the major decision you recorded in chapter 1, did you over- or under-utilize your special design as you made that decision? Are there any ways in which you might approach it differently? How?

3. If you haven't read *LifeKeys* or done a similar self-discovery process, work through Appendix A. Are you surprised that any of the things you do are considered gifts? Which ones? When have you made decisions based on what you do well?

4. What parts of your special design seem to be developing, changing, or emerging right now? What do you think it might mean?

5. The root of the word *enthusiasm* is *en theos*, which means "with God." Thus passions could be described as things we do enthusiastically, with God. What are your major activities right now? Work? Family? Volunteer responsibilities? What in your life are you truly passionate about? Are there things on which you'd rather work *en theos*, with God? Is God telling you anything through passions that are shifting in importance? Work through the questions on page 74.

6. Reflect on Genesis 1:26-27, Psalm 139:13-16, Ephesians 2:10. Do you believe you are uniquely created in God's image to do good works that God has planned for you? Which verse is easiest for you to believe? Which is hardest? Why?

Experiencing God's Guidance Through Your Special Design

At the end of each chapter that describes one of God's four guidance systems is a page, much like this one, to help you apply the system to a specific decision in your life. Appendix C also contains a complete set of these pages, which you may copy for other decisions, as well as a sample summary page to aid you in integrating the information you gain from all of the systems.

Note: Working through a personal discovery process such as *LifeKeys* will enhance your ability to understand how God might be guiding you through how you were created.

For this situation, for this decision, or for today, my special, God-given design (gifts, personality, values, passions) seems to be providing me with guidance in the following ways:

Life Gifts and Spiritual Gifts

Alternative choices I have	Gifts I believe are needed for each choice	Do I have this gift?	What is God saying about my choices through how I am gifted?

Psychological Type: As I review the places or atmospheres that best fit my type, what guidance might God be providing about my choices?

How might my psychological type help/hinder this decision? (see pages 82–83).

Passions and Interests: Ignoring the "practical" considerations for a moment, what are my passions or interests right now? Are they changing? Is God trying to lead me toward something new I might do *en theos,* enthusiastically with God?

Values: What values, beliefs, principles, etc., are core to me in this situation? Which can't be overlooked? Am I paying attention to the values God wants me to hold today for this decision?

Guidance System #3

Scripture

Circumstances   ←→   God's Will   ←→   Special Design

Spirit
direct leadings from
the Holy Spirit that
come in many forms

Chapter 4

Does God Ever Speak Directly?
Listening to the Holy Spirit

While he was still speaking, suddenly a bright cloud
overshadowed them, and from the cloud a voice said,
"This is my Son, the Beloved; with him I am well pleased;
listen to him!"

—Matthew 17:5 NRSV

Before you read this chapter, think about:

1. How would you rank your comfort with finding God's guidance through the Holy Spirit? Use a scale of 1 ("I'm not sure if this works") to 10 ("I'm very comfortable with this form of God's guidance").

2. How do you think this piece of God's system for finding God's will works best? What questions do you have about it?

3. What are your biggest worries or fears about listening for the Holy Spirit to find God's guidance for your life?

On its first migration flight, a young trumpeter swan gets to follow the flock. While its navigation systems seem to be in place from birth, the cygnet flies with an assurance that comes from not having to be the leader. Eventually, it will be one of the elders of the flock, confident of the way. But on that first journey to its winter grounds, the cygnet doesn't have to worry about getting lost. As long as it stays in formation, the adult swans will take the lead.

Does God ever lead us directly? Does God ever "get out in front of us" in a way that's so obvious that all we have to do is follow?

> "And I will ask the Father, and he will give you another Counselor to be with you forever—the Spirit of truth. The world cannot accept him, because it neither sees him nor knows him. But you know him, for he lives with you and will be in you" (John 14:16-17).

> "But when he, the Spirit of truth, comes, he will guide you into all truth. He will not speak on his own; he will speak only what he hears, and he will tell you what is yet to come" (John 16:13).

> This is what we speak, not in words taught us by human wisdom but in words taught by the Spirit, expressing spiritual truths in spiritual words. (1 Corinthians 2:13)

> Now it is God who makes both us and you stand firm in Christ. He anointed us, set his seal of ownership on us, and put his Spirit in our hearts as a deposit, guaranteeing what is to come. (2 Corinthians 1:21-22)

Thus, the Bible tells us that the Holy Spirit
(a) is inside of us;
(b) is known as the Spirit of truth;
(c) is with us forever;
(d) will guide us into all truth;
(e) will tell us what is yet to come.
Christians would agree that the Spirit guides us by helping us understand how the teachings of the Bible apply to us indi-

vidually. But do you believe that God still speaks to people directly? That is, in the way God did in the Old Testament: "So God said to Noah, 'I am going to put an end to all people...make yourself an ark of cypress wood'" (Genesis 6:13-14); and "God said to Moses, 'I AM WHO I AM. This is what you are to say to the Israelites: "I AM has sent me to you"'" (Exodus 3:14). God didn't leave much room for doubt. Noah built the ark, and Moses went back to Egypt to lead the Israelites. Does God speak to you that way?

Some Christians say *always*. They believe that God speaks so clearly that we are to wait for unmistakable signs. When we are convinced we know the will of God, it is time to act, and not before. While this is sometimes true, we have seen three problems arise from this approach:

1. People who hold this position often ignore the other guidance systems. Because they are looking for a *direct* sign, they may miss what God has already told them in the Bible about the situation—or what God is saying through how they are gifted or through the counsel of others. One of our colleagues once gave a career-planning seminar to a group of professional athletes. A football player made it clear from the start, "I don't need any of this. I don't have to plan my future. God will show me what I'm to do when I'm done playing football." We can't help but think that God could guide this individual a little more easily if he at least perused his gifts and talents to narrow down the 12,000-plus kinds of jobs the Department of Labor claims exist!

   People who only look for direct guidance may also start seeing signs when there are none. One young man was certain that God wanted him to become a minister because he saw crosses everywhere he looked. Try this: look around the room where you are now. If you concentrate on looking for crosses, how many do you see? Ceiling and floor tiles, windowpanes, bookshelves, cabinets. The same thing will happen if you are debating between buying two different cars—you'll start seeing similar ones everywhere. However, the crosses, the cars, were always there. Now you've just conditioned yourself to see them. Maybe the man is supposed to be a minister, but take his reasoning too seriously and we'll all be applying for seminary!

To us, waiting for a direct sign is rather like trying to do a school assignment without reading the directions. Good teachers send students back to their seats to read the directions if their questions can be resolved by doing so. They don't do the work for the student. God gave you directions in the form of Scripture and your design that can be read before you start looking for clear guidance. If our cross-spotting young man evaluated his gifts and passions and still felt called to ministry, he'd have a much sounder basis for his decision.

2. Concentrating on direct leadings may also cause us to fall into the trap of demanding certainty when God is asking you to step out in faith. A friend of a friend of ours, a seminary graduate, has been waiting tables for years rather than accept any one of a number of calls to be a pastor because he assumes that God would guide him directly on anything so important. He's chosen inaction rather than looking to any of the other guidance systems to help him make a decision.

A better interpretation might be that God trusts him with the choice. When all of our choices are within God's will, God may rely on our judgment. Think of situations, as an adolescent, when you were allowed to make choices: which instrument to play, which sport to try out for, which books to read, as long as you displayed good judgment. God seems to act in the same way. In fact, in the book of Acts, Paul received the most sensational forms of guidance as a beginning Christian. Later, as he matured in his faith, the text doesn't explain *how* the Spirit communicated to Paul. Paul seemed to be walking so closely with God that God could direct him quietly: "And now, compelled by the Spirit, I am going to Jerusalem" (Acts 20:22).

Paul's own words also confirm that we have choices, that the right thing to do isn't always black and white: "For to me, to live is Christ and to die is gain. If I am to go on living in the body, this will mean fruitful labor for me. Yet what shall I *choose*?" (Philippians 1:21-22, emphasis added).

3. Relying on direct guidance can make people more susceptible to false leadings: "God told me to do it" has been said all too often in courts of law because people can be so certain of what they've been told that they don't check it against biblical wisdom or seek counsel from other Christians.

At the other extreme, people who declare that God *never* guides us directly ignore the truth that the Holy Spirit is already within us to guide us. Perhaps because they've seen the sensational side of this guidance system so misused, they choose to ignore concrete experiences others have had where the Spirit got their attention. Or, they may habitually march ahead without consulting others or trying to discover what God might be doing or saying to them. Prayer may not be a regular part of their decision process; they may be experienced enough in some areas of their lives to think that they don't need God's guidance. Whatever the reasons, they shut themselves off to this guidance system.

While we can certainly rely on past experience and our knowledge of biblical wisdom for decisions about everyday life, the Bible shows a pattern of people continuing to ask for guidance even in situations similar to those they've seen before. If Jesus and Paul and David continued to seek guidance, we probably shouldn't rely only on what's worked before. Why close ourselves to the possibility of direct guidance for an important decision?

As you've surmised, we take the middle ground in this issue: God *sometimes* leads us directly. If we expect an unmistakable sign for every decision we face, we're asking for more certainty than the Bible promises. Remember, when Moses was trying to identify the spirit speaking from the burning bush, God told Moses that he would only be *sure* it was God *after* he'd done everything God had told him to. The assurance came after obedience, not before. Jesus, too, warned against insistence upon signs: "Then some of the Pharisees and teachers of the law said to him, 'Teacher, we want to see a miraculous sign from you.' He answered, 'A wicked and adulterous generation asks for a miraculous sign!'" (Matthew 12:38-39).

While the apostles sometimes received direct guidance, there are plenty of examples in the book of Acts where they traveled, preached, healed, and ministered without a sign, simply acting on the mission they believed they'd been given. The Holy Spirit can direct our lives toward the truth. To help you see how this guidance system works, let's start with the who, what, why, when, and how of this system.

Who Is the Holy Spirit?

"But the Counselor, the Holy Spirit, whom the Father will send in my name, will teach you all things and will remind you of everything I have said to you" (John 14:26).

Grasping who the Holy Spirit *is* can be more difficult than understanding what the Holy Spirit *does.* The Greek word being translated is *paraclete,* and can be literally rendered as "one at hand" or "one alongside to help" or "one who may be counted upon in any emergency." William Barclay describes the function of the Holy Spirit as filling a person "with that Spirit of power and courage which would make him able triumphantly to cope with life."[1] Different translations refer to the Holy Spirit as

- Counselor
- Helper
- Friend
- Comforter
- Spirit of Truth

The Holy Spirit, then, walks alongside us, helps us, counsels us, comforts us, all in an effort to help us to know God and focus on truth. Jesus describes the Holy Spirit as the equivalent of his physical presence with the disciples:

"If you love me, you will keep my commandments. And I

---

1 William Barclay, *New Testament Words* (Philadelphia: The Westminster Press, 1974), 216.

will ask the Father, and he will give you another Advocate, to be with you forever. This is the Spirit of truth, whom the world cannot receive, because it neither sees him nor knows him. You know him, because he abides with you, and he will be in you. I will not leave you orphaned; I am coming to you" (John 14:15-18 NRSV).

Those who love God have the Holy Spirit within them to act as a guide. The eighteenth-century Quaker Hanna Whitall Smith tells us:

> God's way of working, therefore, is to get possession of the inside of a man, to take the control and management of his will, and to work it for him. Then obedience is easy and a delight, and service becomes perfect freedom, until the Christian is forced to explain, "This happy service! who could dream earth had such liberty?"[2]

If you could get inside the head of another person (and what parent hasn't longed to do so with a child?), wouldn't it be easy to point out what to do and why you believe that course of action is best? That's God's plan for guiding us through the Holy Spirit.

What Should We Be Looking For?

From the inside out, then, God is trying to get our attention or focus it properly. Some of God's messages are subtle, some are obvious. Some are sent to comfort us or provide assurance that we are walking with God, some are sent to provide courage, as our very faith may be challenged by what is occurring in our lives. It happens—and we can look for God as long as we're checking the other guidance systems. But be careful that your craving for certainty doesn't block you from the messages of the other three—or that using Scripture, your special design, and circumstances, doesn't keep you from hearing the Holy Spirit.

In the Bible, many of the people who were guided by loud-

---

2 Hanna Whitall Smith, *The Christian's Secret of a Happy Life* (Old Tappan, N.J.: Fleming H. Revell Company, 1952), 189.

and-clear instructions were about to be involved in extraordinary events. Or, they needed reassurance or hope after something they experienced. They weren't asking for direct guidance, although they were open to it. In big ways and small, the Holy Spirit guided them when the other three systems weren't enough.

All of us yearn for physical signs, and God frequently seems to provide them when people need them most. We know of one woman who, at a low point in her career, headed outside for lunch one day just to hear the noontime church bells ring to remind her that God really loved her. That day (and she's never discovered why) the bells rang not only the usual twelve but more than two dozen times! However, in the Bible the most unmistakable physical signs often came when people weren't paying attention in the first place to what God was saying. If you're a slow learner like Paul, you might be blinded and knocked from a horse. Doubt what a bona fide angel tells you, and you might be struck dumb like the father of John the Baptist.

Some of life's decisions are so complicated that we yearn for God to speak directly, to just tell us what to do. Biblically, though, these experiences are rare. People received direct comfort, or certain direction, but they were also asked to conquer the Promised Land, lead troops into battle, or be the next prophet. However, you might hear God's voice in the still of the night, as Samuel did when God called him. For most people, God speaks this way when we least expect it, not when we're waiting and hoping it will happen.

There are countless incidences of major guidance from God, but if you count them up, the voice-from-the-clouds, no-mistake-about-it leadings that some Christians crave daily are biblically reserved for crucial moments—either in the life of an individual or the church—not common decisions that God has already provided guidance for through our special design or Scripture. And while the people of the Bible received guidance throughout their lives, many experienced spectacular guidance at the beginning of their close walk with God; later, God could get their attention in more quiet ways.

God *does* speak to us, but quite often the direct leadings of God are less dramatic than what we are looking for. Even in the Bible, some of the clearest accounts of God's leadings are quiet:

> The Lord said, "Go out and stand on the mountain in the presence of the Lord, for the Lord is about to pass by." Then a great and powerful wind tore the mountains apart and shattered the rocks before the Lord, but the Lord was not in the wind. After the wind there was an earthquake, but the Lord was not in the earthquake. After the earthquake came a fire, but the Lord was not in the fire. And after the fire came a gentle whisper. When Elijah heard it, he pulled his cloak over his face and went out and stood at the mouth of the cave. Then a voice said to him, "What are you doing here, Elijah?" (1 Kings 19:11-13).

All too often, we're hoping for a sign from God as obvious as the wind, quake, or fire when God has been whispering to us all along. Why just a whisper? Because we're supposed to be trusting in God, praying without ceasing, seeking God with all our heart, acknowledging the Lord in all our ways, and asking for wisdom. And if we are doing so, God doesn't have to shout.

Gideon learned how to listen to God (although God sent angels to convince Gideon of his first big tasks). He figured out that God was with him after overhearing a simple conversation. (See Judges 7:13.)

Samuel learned to listen for God from a voice so ordinary that he assumed it was his master Eli calling.

Noah learned how to listen, too. He knew it was safe to get out of the ark from the sight of an olive leaf in the beak of a dove. (See Genesis 8:10-11.)

The Magi saw a sign in the stars that countless others missed.

Okay, you say, so almost anything could be the voice of God. Kooks find God in the tea leaves, too. Let us emphasize again that this is only one of four guidance systems. And, from what we can tell, God uses it in different ways with different people. One person may often have dreams while others may find themselves staring at something in nature, realizing that God is trying to get their attention. Others may not hear voices, but be startled into action by something they read or hear.

Don't be too quick to judge what other people believe is God speaking to them.

And please don't dismiss the chances of it happening to you.

As long as people are checking what they believe might be a direct leading against the other three guidance systems, allow them to explore whether the Holy Spirit is communicating with them.

Why Does the Holy Spirit Guide Us Directly?

While direct guidance is one of the greatest mysteries of the God whose ways are not our ways, we've found several consistencies concerning guidance through the Holy Spirit. Probably the most significant is this: *God frequently uses direct leadings of the Spirit in combination with at least one of the other three guidance systems. The two extremes to avoid are always waiting for a direct leading and never bothering to ask for direct guidance.* This guidance system is no more or less valid than the other three systems. But in developing your use of the systems, it won't be the first you master. Heeding the guidance of the Spirit can be tough, because for God to speak to you directly:

- You have to be able to recognize the voice of God. Direct leadings will not violate the moral will of God as expressed in the Bible. Knowing that moral will, helps you to interpret direct leadings. Further, you can waste a lot of time searching for an unmistakable sign when the Bible may contain the answer all along.

- You have to recognize the differences in how each of us is created, for the Holy Spirit communicates differently with different people. Take the two of us, for example:

    Jane: *I've always trusted the insights I receive through prayer and study, but it took me awhile to recognize that many of those insights came directly from God. God tends to speak to me quietly, when I glean something from a familiar passage of Scripture that I hadn't noticed before or when an idea comes to me that is simply too useful for me to have unearthed it on* my own. When I finally recognized God in these incidents, I began to ask directly for help in this way. These prayers are almost always answered quickly.

The other common experience I have is a feeling that God is holding my tongue, helping me listen to what someone else is saying—and at the same time I hear what God wants me to say to that person. This usually happens when I need to recognize one of my faults or my share of the blame in a difficult situation. After a couple of clear experiences of this during my years as a financial analyst, I learned to ask God to guard how I responded.

In other words, the more I started looking for God's direct leadings, the more I became aware of them in my life. I don't see visions or hear voices, rather I feel quietly guided from within, as if the Holy Spirit is directing my attention to certain things in the environment or my thoughts to definite conclusions.

David: *Actually, those who know me best understand that I'm a flaming "Presbycostal." My first Christian experiences were with a charismatic group, so I leaned toward the extreme of looking only for direct leadings. Once as an associate pastor, I was convinced that God had told me I would become the senior pastor. It didn't happen, but I learned a key lesson: If I think I've experienced a direct leading, I need to test it against the other guidance systems. In this incident, I would have learned quickly that because of past experiences, the church's governing board had an unbendable policy that associate pastors would never assume the leadership role.*

I frequently have rather "loud" experiences of direct leadings. Sometimes I hear an audible voice telling me to go somewhere or do something. Other times I've seen images that seem to contain messages, which often later prove to be God-given. But I no longer act on these by themselves. They may be authentic, but sometimes either I've misinterpreted the message or the source simply wasn't God.

How often does this guidance system operate? You don't need any special guidance to simply do the will of God. Obey the commandments. Love God above all else and your neighbor as yourself. However, the direct leadings often help us see specifically how we are to carry out these directions. In other words, the Bible might tell us to feed the poor, but a dream or image might guide you to volunteer at a soup kitchen or organize a Thanksgiving food drive or fix dinners for a working single parent in your apartment building.

Remember, God is trying to make it as easy as possible for us to discover what we are supposed to do. That's why we have the Bible; that's why we have the promise that we were created with good works in mind. But God knows that this isn't always enough. We sometimes don't see what these forms of guidance are showing because:

- What we see in the world is colored by our lack of understanding, so these more direct forms of guidance help bring things into focus. "Now we see things imperfectly as in a poor mirror, but then we will see everything with perfect clarity. All that I know now is partial and incomplete, but then I will know everything completely, just as God knows me now" (1 Corinthians 13:12 NLT).
- Even when we do see things clearly, we often miss the point of it all. "For my thoughts are not your thoughts, neither are your ways my ways," declares the Lord. "As the heavens are higher than the earth, so are my ways higher than your ways and my thoughts than your thoughts" (Isaiah 55:8-9).

Adding this guidance to the others enables you to understand more easily what God wants you to do. People who operate easily in this guidance system learn to trust it even for the little things in life. Jane, for example, may still forget to pray, but when she remembers she finds that God helps bring to mind sources for anecdotes and quotes, people she might interview for stories, insights for how to deal with her children, even the location of a book or file she needs (and she is excellent at misplacing things!). You can put it all down to more organized thinking once she stops rushing around, but for Jane, it feels more like an instant telegram from God.

While these examples deal with seemingly insignificant things in the scheme of life, God cares about the details of our lives. Author Catherine Marshall studied how to know when her inner feelings were actually the Holy Spirit guiding her. She acknowledged that inner direction should be checked out with fellow Christians and what is said in Scripture. "However, I found that in the everydayness of life when there was not time for this more thorough checking, and when the inner guidance did not obviously violate any of God's loving laws or hurt another, it was important to obey and thus experiment with it. That was how I learned to recognize the Helper's voice."[3]

You can look for this form of guidance, then, in both the little and the big matters of life. However, if God is going to show you *exactly* what to do, it will probably be for the next one or two steps into the future, not a full blueprint of the next five years. For example, the Israelites knew that eventually the Promised Land would be theirs, but God only gave the battle plans to Joshua one at a time.

You might have a sudden, compelling vision of yourself as a small group leader, the owner of a start-up business, a Christian gospel singer, the holder of a new patent, a crisis center counselor, or a Habitat for Humanity coordinator. (Remember, this form of guidance operates alongside the others—check the vision against how you are fearfully and wonderfully made!) Even so, the vision may be no more specific than a destination. The decisions about where to seek training or employment may be left up to you. Or you may know instantly who you are to contact or where you might work first, but not be given any further hints as to where this road might take you.

I was sure that God told me my work as an associate pastor at a California church was over when the senior pastor left— and I felt just as strongly that I was to move to the Pacific Northwest. While I believed the idea came from God, it still seemed crazy. God didn't give a clue as to what town to go to

---

3 Catherine Marshall, *The Helper* (Grand Rapids, Mich.: Chosen Books, 1978), 91.

*or whether I'd even continue in the ministry, but my wife agreed
that it seemed to be the right choice, and we moved.*

*Two small churches near our new home were searching for a
pastor, and I found employment immediately.*

—Mitch, 44, pastor

*I applied to both Princeton and Fuller for seminary, but felt
that Fuller would be a better match for my theology. However,
when I received acceptances from both, my mind filled with
images of Princeton—I'd once hoped to go there to study polit-
ical science. My wife, Janet, and I traveled out east, not sure how
we'd even support ourselves if Princeton seemed the right choice.
The atmosphere seemed right, but even more affirming was that
Janet immediately found a job as a dietitian, her specialty.*

—David

While you probably wouldn't want to step out before checking a vision with other mature Christians and with the wisdom of the Bible, that doesn't mean that God won't sometimes ask you to step out in faith. The guidance of the Holy Spirit
may not make sense at first. For example, even with the vision
Peter had of the clean and unclean animals being brought
together, he certainly had no idea why God had asked him to
go to the home of a Gentile with whom he wasn't supposed to
associate (Acts 10). Paul didn't know what would happen when
he followed his dream over to Macedonia (Acts 16:9). Philip, as
he watched the approaching chariot, didn't know he was about
to convert its owner to Christianity (Acts 8:26-35). But Peter,
Paul, and Philip charged ahead anyway.

Not only may you have to step out in faith, but you may still
have doubts and you may not like the way God is telling you
to go! You might feel like Jonah, who may have gone to Nineveh
once God got his attention in the belly of the whale, but still
complained bitterly that the Ninevites were being given an unfair
break.

When Does God Lead Us Directly?

While God may lead directly in both the big and the small decisions of our lives, this guidance system operates most frequently in the more specific cases.

When we are about to face danger. The most obvious example is in the Christmas story. Both the wise men and Joseph were warned in dreams to get out of Herod's path. Sometimes God lets us know that the bottom is about to drop out just so we can believe that our Creator still cares about us. Jesus told Peter that in his old age he would be led where he did not want to go. Paul was warned in advance that going to Jerusalem would bring trouble.

When God wants to give us knowledge about a situation that we couldn't otherwise have, which will help us or another person. Sometimes God wants to warn us in advance, like making sure Ananias knew that it was *the* Saul he'd be talking to. God gave Ananias a chance to ask questions (so Ananias could understand that God wasn't crazy!).

> *I attended a conference in a town where I used to live and arranged to meet with several of my old colleagues for lunch. One of them kept staring at me and finally asked, "David, have you had any medical problems? Is there something wrong with your stomach?" When I said I was fine, she paused for a moment, and then said, "I get it now. God wants you to know that when you go back home, events are going to erupt that will make you feel like you've been hit in the stomach. But God will be with you."*
>
> *What she believed God had told her came to pass, but as I walked through those moments, I looked for God's presence and was comforted by the foreknowledge I'd received.*
>
> —Dave

When the Holy Spirit wants to change our desires or beliefs.
Clearly, on the road to Damascus, Jesus spoke directly to Paul to
change this foremost prosecutor of the church into its biggest
promoter. Many of the church's most influential figures had similar experiences:

- John Wesley, even though he was the son of a pastor and
  a devout Christian, didn't really understand what it meant
  to be loved by God until at a prayer meeting, listening to
  Luther's introduction to the book of Galatians, his "heart
  was strangely warmed." His subsequent fervor solidified
  the movement that became the Methodist Church.
- Teresa of Avila prayed to better understand what it meant
  to have a strong inner life with God. As she prayed, the
  image came to her of a castle. Her writings on our souls
  as castles worthy of being home to Christ have influenced
  Christians for more than four hundred years.
- Blaise Pascal, a French mathematician and theologian, went
  from doubter to a great defender of Christianity after simply hearing a sermon.

But this also happens to "ordinary" Christians.

> I had successfully taught adult education classes for years, but
> when our church held all adult education classes off site because
> of crowded facilities, attendance dwindled. I felt I was wasting
> my time teaching to so few. Not only was I ready to give up on
> teaching, but I began to wonder whether another church might
> be better able to use my gifts. Deeply discouraged, I was pray-
> ing about these matters one Sunday as I entered the sanctuary
> for worship, when I felt the Lord speak to me, "If you don't teach,
> how will they be fed?" Attendance didn't change, but my enthu-
> siasm returned.
>
> —Tom, 40, nonprofit executive

When we need a special provision of God's love. Sometimes
God knows we need a push or a special measure of certainty.
Some of these might be:

- When someone is very new to the Gospel message or if life circumstances have caused bitter doubts to arise.
- When people have perhaps begun to wither under the weight of circumstances.
- When we need something to tuck away for the rest of our lives and pull out again when we need a reminder of how great God really is. A steady diet of miracles or signs doesn't help make us better Christians—or the Israelites would have done a whole lot better at obeying God in the wilderness. But when handled properly, a single "mountaintop" experience can serve as a for-all-time reminder of God's constant presence.
- When persecution is rampant and we need encouragement.
- When something unbelievable is about to happen and the Holy Spirit acts as a messenger so we have no doubt that the miracle is from God.
- When the directions God wants to give us are specific and not easily determined otherwise. For example, when God revealed to Samuel that Saul was to be the first king of Israel, the choice seemed obvious: tall and handsome, Saul looked like a king. However, David's big brothers all looked at least as kingly as David, the shepherd boy. God was with Samuel during every moment of that visit in Jesse's house. When David finally came in from the hills, God said, "That's the one. Anoint him."

When someone hasn't taken the first, second, third, or fourth hints that God wants something done. These are the belly-of-the-whale/road-to-Damascus types of experiences that we should all strive to avoid by learning to listen for God the first time. Paul, for example, heard Stephen's powerful speech about how Israel persecuted prophet after prophet, their hearts hardened toward God. Apparently, Paul ignored any hint that he might be doing the same thing and simply watched the stones rain down as Stephen died. Jesus had to intervene directly, on the way to Damascus, before Paul changed.

God wants us to practice listening deeply for what the Holy Spirit might be saying. Unless we take an expectant attitude and are open to changing our direction or even our beliefs, it's hard for God to get our attention. In fact, God pleads with us, "So, as the Holy Spirit says, 'Today, if you hear his voice, do not harden your hearts as you did in the rebellion, during the time of testing in the desert'" (Hebrews 3:7-8). Our hearts are to be open to these leadings.

However, if you're listening carefully and hear nothing, don't come to a standstill, paralyzed for lack of a clear sign. Go about your business while remaining receptive. God can find you while you're fishing, collecting taxes, herding sheep, walking down a road, sitting up in a tree, working in the garden—wherever you go, God can meet you there.

How Exactly Are People Led This Way?

It seems that the Holy Spirit tailors direct leadings to what we are most receptive to. These are some of the most common:

Dreams. If you've never had a dream that convinced you of a course of action, the thought of being guided by dreams may seem crazy. For some of you the person who believes in the messages of dreams deserves a diagnosis of insanity—and we agree if they aren't checking those dreams against the other guidance systems.

But the Bible makes clear that dreams are a valid source of guidance; many cultures around the world consider it foolish to disregard their messages. Dreams may chase you to safety in Egypt, like Joseph and Mary; or help you to recognize God in the midst of adversity, like Jacob as he fled Esau's wrath; or warn of catastrophe so those who heed them can be ready themselves for what is to come; but the dreams of the Bible don't concern everyday decisions.

Sometimes these dreams simply help us become aware of feelings we've been burying about a situation. Jane decided to give one of her children an extra year before starting kindergarten after she had several nightmares about what that child might experience as the youngest in the class.

Biblically, though, dreams can be much more direct. Both Joseph and Daniel were promoted because of their abilities to interpret the symbolism of dreams. The Magi relied on dreams to guide their actions. God used a dream to assure Joseph that he should take Mary as his wife. And listen to these modern examples:

Janet, David's wife, accepted his proposal of marriage, but they agreed to pray for a month before announcing their engagement. The next morning Janet's best friend said, "I dreamed you were engaged—why didn't you tell me?"

One of David's college professors taught logically and clearly about the kingdom of God, but struggled with applying faith to his personal life. He had a recurring dream about running to catch a train and then not having a valid ticket. When he related his dream to some friends, they suggested that he didn't have a ticket because he hadn't turned his life over to God—this insight gave him the courage to take that step.

At this point you may be thinking, "But God doesn't speak to me this way. Am I out of favor, unable to listen, or too deep a sleeper?" Truly, God doesn't guide some people this way to make the rest of us feel less spiritual. Instead, we believe the Holy Spirit guides each one of us gently and respectfully in the ways we can best understand. Chances are you've been led and not recognized God's hand in it.

People. You may be out for coffee with a friend or listening to a sermon. And suddenly the words you hear convince you of something you should do.

While I seldom recognize God in a person immediately, after most crises in my life, I look back to realize that God had someone walk beside me. For example, during a particularly rough time in college, I foolishly agreed to play French horn for a musical. Stuck in rehearsals from 6:00-12:00 every night on top of a nightmarish class schedule, I was crabby, tired, and afraid of flunking chemistry. I isolated myself from my friends but couldn't avoid the bassoon player next to me at all of those rehearsals. He had the best sense of humor and laughed me out of what was bordering on a nervous breakdown. Keith turned out to be a strong Christian. Somehow our banter helped me get things back into perspective.

If that were the only time I'd been helped this way, I might pass it off as coincidence, but God seems to make it the rule, not the exception, to place beside me a person who has just the wisdom and faith I need to learn from.

—Jane

Images. The Bible is full of examples in which God gives people an image to clarify a message. For example, one incident from Jeremiah:

> This is the word that came to Jeremiah from the Lord: "Go down to the potter's house, and there I will give you my message."
>
> So I went down to the potter's house, and I saw him working at the wheel. But the pot he was shaping from the clay was marred in his hands; so the potter formed it into another pot, shaping it as seemed best to him.
>
> Then the word of the Lord came to me: "'O house of Israel, can I not do with you as this potter does?' declares the Lord. 'Like clay in the hand of the potter, so are you in my hand, O house of Israel'" (Jeremiah 18:1-6).

While God can guide any of us this way, some people seem to be more attentive to situations so that God can speak to them. If you have the gift of prophecy, you may commonly experience God's wisdom or direction in this manner. And note that if Jeremiah hadn't obeyed by going to the potter's house, God couldn't have given him the image.

One of our friends was asked to head up a stewardship campaign, always a difficult task. As he prayed over how to reach people's hearts instead of just going for their pocketbooks, he received a clear image of tightly clenched fists. During his talk on giving, he asked people to make a fist and hold it, then feel the relief of relaxing that grip. He then made the analogy of the relief we can feel when we no longer need to clutch so tightly to our resources.

Another friend was considering moving his family to another state, leaving his job to start a new ministry. A prayer partner said, "All I can picture is you and your family in a boat that is only half-built." As they prayed about it, they both felt that the boat meant that the family wasn't ready for such a major change.

But visions can look like a lot of things: how a system should be organized, how a car should be rebuilt, how a rock collection might be categorized, how a story might come to life, how a team might accomplish something, how a law might change or prevent things.

Perhaps you don't think you've had an experience like this. That may be so, but you may also not have recognized a thought or image as coming from God. It may be that God speaks to you in other ways, but it may also be that "You do not have, because you do not ask God" (James 4:2). Again, if you aren't receptive, God can't guide you this way.

Prophecies. Meeting a prophet can be a bit unnerving—do you really want to know what God thinks of you or your church or our society or the state of the world in general?

But prophecies are as much about encouragement as they are about correction. Biblically, prophecies point out whether or not we are aligned with God's will. Yes, they sometimes dealt with the future, but it was often in terms of "Israel, if you don't turn back to God, then this will happen."

> On a matter very dear to me, I left a meeting incensed because I was sure the leader had manipulated the voting. That same week, I met with friends, one of whom has the gift of prophecy. She said she'd had a vision. "You're really upset about a decision someone over you has made. You need to know that God knows about this and there will be an opportunity for you to let your thoughts be known." With the reassurance that I'd have another chance to air my views, I was able to continue working with the committee.

Sure enough, a few weeks later, someone with more clout than me asked that we reconsider. I carefully made my point and our leader took it into consideration, saying, "I have to think about it, but perhaps I'm feeling a lot more pride than spirituality."
—David

Prophecies, then, can show us where to go or simply give us the confidence to keep moving.

Angels. Angels can bring messages of comfort or of warning. Biblically, angels appear to inform people of roles they are about to play, to execute God's judgment, to protect and rescue God's people, to warn them of mission-threatening dangers, and to worship God. Angels often come when God wants people to know with certainty that they will be able to accomplish the impossible, e.g., conquer invaders (Gideon), have children past childbearing years (Abraham and Sarah, Zechariah and Elizabeth), bear the Son of God (Mary), take an unpopular message to a king (Elijah)—angels are sometimes God's shield for our faith when the stakes are high and the opposition formidable.

Now an angel of the Lord said to Philip, "Go south to the road—the desert road—that goes down from Jerusalem to Gaza" (Acts 8:26).

At Caesarea there was a man named Cornelius, a centurion in what was known as the Italian Regiment. He and all his family were devout and God-fearing; he gave generously to those in need and prayed to God regularly. One day at about three in the afternoon he had a vision. He distinctly saw an angel of God, who came to him and said, "Cornelius!"
Cornelius stared at him in fear. "What is it, Lord?" he asked. The angel answered, "Your prayers and gifts to the poor have come up as a memorial offering before God. Now send men to Joppa to bring back a man named Simon who is called Peter" (Acts 10:1-5).

Suddenly an angel of the Lord appeared and a light shone in the cell. He struck Peter on the side and woke him up.

"Quick, get up!" he said, and the chains fell off Peter's wrists. Then the angel said to him, "Put on your clothes and sandals." And Peter did so. "Wrap your cloak around you and follow me," the angel told him. Peter followed him out of the prison, but he had no idea that what the angel was doing was really happening; he thought he was seeing a vision. (Acts 12:7-9)

Perhaps you have never seen an angel; perhaps you have but didn't recognize it as such. Some of the more credible accounts have a few things in common: the circumstances required instant or unusual guidance, the person wasn't looking for anything out of the ordinary, and in some way, what happened conveyed God's love to the person.

> *Back in the 1970s, when perhaps we weren't so acutely aware of how dangerous the world is, I spent a summer in Paris. Walking down a busy boulevard, I struck up a conversation with a seemingly nice young man. He said he was a medical student and offered to show me the Sacre Coeur by night, something I had longed to see. As we headed down the steps of the subway station, I chanced to look up. Standing above me, a man leaned over the railing, shaking his head "no." So I changed my mind and didn't go. Later, I realized how dangerous the situation might have become.*
>
> —Binnie, 70, counselor

Was the person she saw an angel? Certainly no human knew that she was walking with a total stranger. As with all forms of guidance, checking what we believe against the criteria of the Bible and the other guidance systems is the best protection against being misled by unholy angels. In her book *All About Angels*, Jill Hartman suggests that to test such an experience we ask ourselves,

- Does this experience stand up to what the Bible teaches about angels?
- Did it provide protection, comfort, or direction that can't be explained by a natural source?
- Did it point us toward God? Angel experiences won't take us from God, but will move us to offer praise and glory.

- Did it cause a powerful emotional response, perhaps of fear or peace?[4]

Direct commands. God still gives the sort of "Get thee to Nineveh" direct commands that left Jonah quaking in his sandals. Sometimes, as discussed above, these commands direct us toward something huge that God wants done. In the book of Acts, people often received direct commands from God:

> In Damascus there was a disciple named Ananias. The Lord called to him in a vision, "Ananias!"
> "Yes, Lord," he answered.
> The Lord told him, "Go to the house of Judas on Straight Street and ask for a man from Tarsus named Saul, for he is praying" (Acts 9:10-11).

Other times, the command involves a small, but perhaps consequential, thing that God wants us to do.

> *During prayer time, I'm occasionally convinced that God has spoken to me. However, God waits until I give up my own ego. Only then am I genuinely led so that clarity comes. Unless I manage to tame the storms inside, I don't receive clear direction.*
>
> *But if I do, the commands can be unmistakable. One morning, God distinctly said, "Go to the bookstore." Nothing else— and it's a big place. I wasn't even sure which section I was supposed to go to. I prayed as I went in the door and the blue spine of a tiny little book caught my eye. Glancing through it, I came up with the structure on which LifeKeys is based.*
>
> *On another occasion, I'd been asked to head a project for my church called "Love Seattle," getting laypeople involved in different projects that would help others see that God loved them. As I prayed about my assignment, God continually pressed upon me to talk to each of the elders of the church. While I didn't hear a direct command, I couldn't escape how important doing so seemed to be. Every elder provided me with a different principle for making the program work: "Make sure you ask not just*

---

4 Jill Hartman, *All About Angels* (St. Louis, Mo.: Concordia Publishing House, 1998), 40.

*what they want to do but what they might add on to what they're
already doing." "Let some of them work in groups and teams,
not just individually." "Be prepared that some will be speaking
out of their brokenness, not their calling."*

*Not only did I heed all of their advice, but I learned the true
role of elders within a church.*

—David

Visions. While an image usually concerns a single object that
somehow conveys a spiritual message, visions may be more
like a motion picture, varying in length from a newsreel spot
to a full-length feature.

> Peter went up on the roof to pray. He became hungry and
> wanted something to eat, and while the meal was being pre-
> pared, he fell into a trance. He saw heaven opened and
> something like a large sheet being let down to earth by its four
> corners. It contained all kinds of four-footed animals, as
> well as reptiles of the earth and birds of the air.
>
> Then a voice told him, "Get up, Peter. Kill and eat."
>
> "Surely not, Lord!" Peter replied. "I have never eaten any-
> thing impure or unclean."
>
> The voice spoke to him a second time, "Do not call anything
> impure that God has made clean." This happened three times,
> and immediately the sheet was taken back to heaven. (Acts
> 10:9-16)

God used this vision to shift a central paradigm the Jewish
people held, that they were forbidden to associate with the
Gentiles.

*I was home on break from graduate school, quite certain
that I wasn't going to continue to pursue a career in horticul-
ture. Walking through a local greenhouse, I had a sudden vision
of myself leading a huge youth ministry. It was so forceful that
I felt compelled to work at that nursery. I asked if they had any
manager positions. Within two weeks, I was out of grad school,
working at the nursery, and volunteering at a local church. While
there, I met my wife, Janet, and decided to go to seminary. I never*

*did do the youth revivals of my vision, but God certainly got
my attention. And I headed in the right direction.*

—David

The vision changed David's general direction, but the specific ways to move in that direction came from the other guidance systems—his circumstances, his gifts and talents, and
biblical study on the role of a pastor.

But Is It Really God Speaking?

Again, God's speaking directly is only one of *four* guidance
systems. Test what you believe God is telling you against the other
three systems. In addition, several things seem to hold true as
you struggle to discern whether God is in the message.

1. The Holy Spirit usually gives us short-term, not long-term
   guidance. Jacob, for example, was confident that he wanted
   to marry Rachel from the time he met her by the well.
   However, he had no idea that his father-in-law would trick him
   into laboring for fourteen years to win her hand. If Jacob
   had known, he might have backed away from the arrangement.
   (See Genesis 29.)

2. Often what we understand seems to be only part of what we
   need, not a complete message. Remember, God's goal is to help
   you become more Christlike. We may only understand enough
   to be convinced of our need to stay close to God. That doesn't
   guarantee a smooth walk, but security that we can reach God's
   goals for us.

   "Whoever serves me must follow me; and where I am, my
   servant also will be. My Father will honor the one who
   serves me.
       Now my heart is troubled, and what shall I say? 'Father, save
   me from this hour'? No, it was for this very reason I came to
   this hour. Father, glorify your name!" (John 12:26-28).

3. We may not understand at first what the Spirit is trying to tell us. Peter was still pondering the vision he'd received when the men Cornelius sent appeared at his door. Only later did he make the connection between the vision and God's desire for him to speak to the Gentiles.

4. Even these direct leadings are open to reason and questioning. If you're not busy cowering in terror at the appearance of an angel (we think that's how we'd react), you can ask questions just as Moses, Mary, Gideon, and Abraham did, to name only a few. Asking the hard questions is normal and acceptable as long as we are willing to listen to God's answers.

5. Direction received from the Holy Spirit will not be out of the moral bounds of God. Now that we've made such a clear-cut statement, we need to qualify it through the eyes of Dietrich Bonhoeffer.

Torn between destroying Hitler, whose government was clearly breaking God's commandments, and personal obedience to the commandment "You shall not murder," few of us would argue that Bonhoeffer acted wrongly in joining the plot to assassinate Hitler. However, before doing so, Bonhoeffer fought the regime through peaceful methods from its beginnings: He was involved in protests from 1933 on; he joined a group seeking to overthrow Hitler in 1938; he decided against seeking refuge in the United States while safely in New York; and he joined the resistance movement, going undercover in the Military Intelligence Department. He was even a delegate to negotiating peace with the Allied Forces, but they insisted on an unconditional surrender. In other words, Bonhoeffer employed every means possible for peaceful resolution before supporting the assassination plot. He also did not act alone, but with others who exhausted all other options before breaking one of God's commandments.

It was hardly a black-and-white decision. And Christians will disagree about his choice, because when our only choices use evil to do away with evil, biblical support can be found for doing evil or doing nothing. For example, two stories in the Bible show God providing opposing wisdom on the very issue of taking the life of a corrupt leader. In 1 Samuel 24, David has a clear chance to kill Saul. His men urge him to do so. After all, David has already been chosen by God as king and Saul is trying to kill him. How much more of an excuse does David need? Yet he refrains from doing so, saying that it was wrong to dishonor someone who had once been annointed by God.

In contrast, in Judges 4 we read the story of the assassination of Sisera. Deborah the prophetess makes it clear that God will deliver Sisera into the hands of the Israelites. The honor of killing Sisera goes to a woman, Jael. We won't even *try* to justify the different outcomes in these stories; our point is, in the Bible, God has asked people to kill and to refrain from killing when evil is present, making similar decisions incredibly difficult to navigate.

6. The guidance you receive may not be for the present moment. It may simply be an encouragement to help you work toward a future. Your question might be, "It's nice to know you're with me, but what am I supposed to do?" and God's answer might be, "Carry on. I just wanted you to understand you're not alone."

7. The Holy Spirit doesn't force us. God wants us to join in willingly, not through coercion. People who've been part of a cult, or the occult, can tell you about the difference. Look at the contrast in the life of the demon-possessed man of the region of the Gerasenes. Before Jesus healed him, he lived among the tombs, crying out at night and cutting himself with stones. Afterward, people were amazed to see him sitting by Jesus, calm, dressed, and in his right mind. In other words, he was back in possession of his faculties (Mark 5).

David once helped counsel a woman who had been involved in channeling spirits in a New Age cult. The spirits began to harass her day and night, trying to force her to harm herself if she didn't comply with their desires for her aid so they could possess others. She finally realized that she was their prisoner, not their willing accomplice.

In *Prince Caspian,* the second volume in C. S. Lewis's THE CHRONICLES OF NARNIA, the children are doing their best to journey across the roughest of terrain to come to Prince Caspian's aid, but can't find any familiar landmarks and are quarreling over which way to go. The majority want to head downstream, the easy route, but Lucy suddenly spots the lion Aslan (who represents Christ) heading up the gorge.

No one believes her. They head the other way, are almost killed by enemy outposts, and have to toil back up the gorge, exhausted and discouraged. That night, while everyone is asleep, Lucy sees Aslan again. She tries to explain to him that no one would believe her.

> "But it wasn't my fault anyway, was it?"
> The lion looked straight into her eyes.
> "Oh Aslan," said Lucy. "You don't mean it was? How could I—I couldn't have left the others and come up to you alone, how could I? Don't look at me like that...oh well, I suppose I could. Yes, and it wouldn't have been alone, I know, not if I was with you...."[5]

Lucy knew then that the guidance had been hers alone to obey. With help from the other guidance systems and sometimes with the counsel of others, each of us is to listen for the Holy Spirit. We may not convince others of the truth of what we've been told, but perhaps they'll come along if we start moving. The author of Hebrews pleads with us, "Therefore God again set a certain day, calling it Today, when a long time later he spoke through David, as was said before: 'Today, if you hear his voice, do not harden your hearts'" (Hebrews 4:7).

---

5 C. S. Lewis, *Prince Caspian* (New York: Macmillan Publishing Company, Collier Books edition, 1970), 137.

Is this the message, Lord?
One foot in front of the other,
Trusting what I know
Yet looking for you?
Help me trust without signs and wonders
But believe them when I see them.
And when you speak my name,
Let my heart hear your voice. Amen.

Reflections for Your Own LifeDirections

1. Look through our main points in this chapter. Which one caught your attention the most? Why?

- The Holy Spirit is already inside of us to guide us into truth.
- Often, God expects us to "do our homework"—applying Scriptures and our special design—before looking for direct leadings.
- Sometimes we want direct leadings when God wants us to step out in faith.
- Direct leadings of the Holy Spirit come in many forms, in different ways, to different people. Often the form honors the needs or personality of the person receiving guidance.
- People often experience more sensational forms of God's guidance either at the start of their spiritual journey or when a great need arises, either personal or in the world around them.

2. Have you experienced direct leadings of the Spirit? Dreams?
   The words or prophecies of other people? Images or visions?
   Angels? Direct commands? Did you know it at the time or did
   you dismiss it?

3. Looking back to the major decision you recorded in chapter 1, did you over- or under-emphasize this guidance system as you evaluated that decision? Are there any ways in which you might approach it differently? How?

4. Have you asked for direct guidance and not received it? Why do you think God might have asked you to rely on the other three systems of guidance?

5. Who do you know who claims to be led this way all the time? Do you envy them or question their judgment? What would you like to ask them about how they use this system? How do you think they discern what is of God and what is not of God?

6. What beliefs or educational training prevent or encourage you to believe in direct guidance? What questions are left over?

Experiencing God's Guidance Through the Spirit

At the end of each chapter that describes one of God's four guidance systems is a page, much like this one, to help you apply the system to a specific decision in your life. Appendix C also contains a complete set of these pages, which you may copy for other decisions, as well as a sample summary page to aid you in integrating the information you gain from all of the systems.

For this situation, for this decision, or for today, God seems to be providing me with direct guidance through the Holy Spirit in the following ways:

Direct Leadings: Have I paid attention to the variety of ways in which God may be trying to get my attention?
• dreams
• the words or prophecies of other people
• images or visions
• angels
• direct commands

What messages might God be giving me through these avenues?

Ideally, how would I like God to direct me for this situation? What further guidance do I need in order to know for certain the choices to make?

Am I erring by either waiting for the certainty the Spirit could provide, ignoring the other guidance systems, or assuming the Spirit won't provide further guidance?

Have I prayed and asked for guidance and wisdom for this decision? What, if any, inputs have come as a result?

Guidance System #4

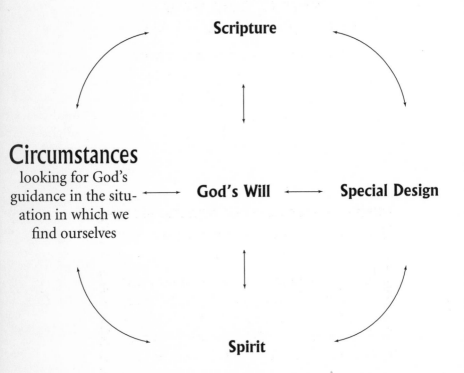

Scripture

Circumstances
looking for God's
guidance in the situ-
ation in which we
find ourselves

God's Will   **Special Design**

Spirit

Chapter 5

What Is Happening in the World Around Me?
Being Guided by Circumstances

The human mind plans the way,
but the Lord directs the steps.

—Proverbs 16:9 NRSV

**Before you read this chapter,
think about:**

1. How would you rank your comfort with finding God's guidance through circumstances? Use a scale of 1 ("I'm not sure if this works") to 10 ("I'm very comfortable with this form of God's guidance.").

2. How do you think this piece of God's system for finding God's will works best? What questions do you have about it?

3. What are your biggest worries or fears about using circumstances to find God's guidance for your life?

If Minnesota nights turn sharply cold and the winds are still *before* the first big snow but *after* most of the leaves are off the trees, the lakes freeze smooth and glasslike. We humans test the ice, lace up our skates, and enjoy the endless expanse of the crystal rink. But ducks don't know that overnight their circumstances have changed. It's hard not to laugh when a whole flock tries to land on what appears to be the same lake they swam in the day before. They slide across the ice, swerving in circles or skidding until they bump into the bank on the other side. Ducks may be able to navigate from north to south as they migrate, but they have no rational thinking process to interpret the reflection of ice to tell them that they need to adapt how they set down.

As children of God, however, we can ask for God's help in interpreting what is happening all around us. This is God's world. While Jesus makes it clear that neither he nor we are of the world (John 17:14-16), we also know that "you, whose name is the Lord—that you alone are the Most High over all the earth" (Psalm 83:18).

Yes, injustice, deception, betrayal, and evil are at work in the world, but God can and does use circumstances to speak to us.

How? Not just by opening or closing doors, but by getting our attention.

Sometimes things happen that seem too unlikely to be coincidental. Some people call these "synchronistic events." While you may hear other interpretations of synchronicity, ours centers on a God whose timing and sovereignty can orchestrate even the smallest details of our lives to get our attention.

Perhaps you've fallen into the trap of if/then thinking. If I get a college degree, then I'll get a better job. If I want to get married, then I'd better go places where I can meet people. If I want to learn to dance, then I should take dancing lessons. If it means more money, then I should take the new job. While all of these thoughts have some validity, you can never control the actions of others, nor can you control all of the circumstances to ensure the outcome. And that reality is often frustrating—but even more so if you thought you had figured out just how your life would go. If you aren't controlling your circumstances, then who is? Richard Hopke, in his book *There Are No Accidents*, puts it this way:

> Ours is a culture that encourages us to believe that we are— or should be—the author of our stories.... Synchronistic events confront us with the fact that sometimes the stories we make up about ourselves, the stories we would like to live, are not necessarily the stories we are actually living or, to go a step further, are meant to live.[1]

Frequently, these synchronistic events happen when we're at a transition point in our lives. Perhaps we're overwhelmed with uncertainty about work, relationships, our children, our health, or a major decision we are facing. Then something happens that seems to either offer comfort, show us our blind spots, or bring into focus the way we should go. Other people might explain away these events, but inside you know they are life-changing.

> *I once volunteered for a retreat team. My group's main job was to pray for the speakers and participants during the four-day event. For the team's first meeting, the ten in my group introduced ourselves to one another. The first woman gave her name and said, "I just left my job as a counselor at a women's crisis center. I needed to recharge after comforting so many victims of abuse."*
>
> *The second team member gave her name and said, "Normally I don't blurt this out, but I just finished two years of therapy after leaving an abusive spouse."*
>
> *The rest of us nodded, but when the third woman on our team added, "I lead support groups for teenage victims of rape," the minister, the only male on the team, said, "I think we need to pay attention to what we have in common. My wife and I just spent two years in therapy helping her work through the sexual abuse her father inflicted. This is too unreal to be coincidental.*

---

[1] Richard N. Hopke, *There Are No Accidents* (New York: Riverhead Books, 1997), 9.

God has brought this team together for a purpose."

During the retreat, our whole group gathered outside the presentation room to hear the only one of fourteen speakers we'd missed during the team meetings. A story the speaker told caused one of the weekenders to have a flashback of sexual abuse. She ran sobbing from the room—right into the arms of the people from my group who knew exactly how to counsel her.

—Jane

While those of us on the team were amazed at God's timing, think of the impact our story had on the weekender for whom God had orchestrated our presence. She received a message she would never forget: God is with her and working to heal her from all the hurt in her past.

"Chance happenings" such as these make us pause to consider how active God is in our lives. Yes, you could figure out the statistical probability of Jane's retreat team having so many counselors, and the percentage chance might even be reasonably high. And perhaps it was just a coincidence that they were sitting outside the door when the woman ran out. And maybe she just needed a hug; any warm words would have served as counsel. But at some point, even the most rational brain has to say, "This explanation is getting too convoluted. Perhaps something bigger happened than I can categorize."

Circumstances like these bypass cause/effect thinking. You move past the facts and pay more attention to how you feel about what happened and how it influenced you. Yes, there might be a perfectly logical explanation, but that isn't the point. You have to take seriously the thought that there might be a deeper meaning to an event than might appear on the surface.

- Jane hadn't felt a real need for serious dating relationships during college. After years of first dates, though, shouldn't you pay more attention when someone you've met only briefly and who knows nothing about you asks you out to your favorite restaurant and little-known theater? It seemed so to Jane, who eventually married this person of great taste.

- Jane debated long and hard about beginning a new career as a writer. On her way to meet with David for the first time about actually devoting time to writing *LifeKeys*, she stopped by a garage sale. On a table were just a few books, but the top one was a famous essay collection on writing, which Jane had wanted to buy but couldn't afford at its retail price. While she continued to research and pray about becoming a writer, purchasing that book for just a dollar was encouraging.

- David had been praying about whether a book on guidance (the book you are holding) might be a good sequel to *LifeKeys* when Jane asked, "What would you think of doing a book on how God guides us?"

- During David's first weeks of graduate school, a friend convinced him to go to an all-campus dance. David's friend said, "You point me toward some girl I'll ask to dance, and I'll point to the girl you have to ask." The girl selected for David happened to be one of the strongest Christians on campus. She invited him to the all-fraternity Bible study. David ended up becoming one of the leaders and discovering his gift of teaching.

Sounds great, doesn't it, to be guided by the events that "randomly" enter our lives? *However, this guidance system isn't quite so simple.*

Avoiding the Traps of Circumstances

Despite the fact that the earth belongs to God, every person who has ever lived has been given the free will to make choices. And the billions of choices that have been made since the birth of humanity have taken the earth a long way away from God's ideal. As you look at whether God is active in the circumstances around you, view the facts through these five realities of life with which we must live:

Our circumstances are part of our experiences in a world that is subject to spiritual warfare. Therefore, our circumstances may or may not reflect the consequences of our actions. Jesus made this clear. When people asked him whether a man had been blind since birth because of his own sins or his parents' sins, Jesus replied that neither was the case. The man was blind so Jesus could heal him and show God's power (John 9:2-3).

However, the reality of spiritual warfare also means that while we may not have caused our situation, the circumstances present do not always have our best interests in mind. King David learned the hard way that just because there's a beautiful woman bathing on the rooftop next to yours doesn't mean you should invite her over. While waiting for Moses to return from Mount Sinai, Aaron learned that just because there is overwhelming popular support for creating a golden calf doesn't mean you should build it. Abraham learned that just because the King of Gerar believes your wife is your sister doesn't mean you should give him her hand in marriage. Circumstances by themselves cannot be used to determine God's will.

Our circumstances aren't the result of our actions alone. For better or worse, your circumstances can be directly affected by those around you as they exercise their free will. This means that even if God is showing you the path to take, someone else may be standing at the fork in the road, blocking your view. What if Johann Sebastian Bach had listened to his jealous older brother, who tried to stifle his musical talents? Or if Helen Keller's parents had agreed with the medical specialists that their daughter couldn't be educated? Or if Margaret Mitchell had believed the editors who rejected *Gone With the Wind* because no one was supposedly interested in Civil War tales?

Our circumstances and, more importantly, what we can do about them may be controlled to some extent by the government, culture, or other worldly systems in which we live and operate. Picture for a moment how different your options are for dealing with unemployment in the United States compared to

Jamaica, where the jobless rate hovers around 60 percent. Or for worshiping God in Communist Cuba.

Our circumstances take place within the body of Christ. That means that you can look to other Christians for help in interpreting your situation. However, always take the counsel of others into the waiting room of your soul. Listen carefully to their advice and try to understand each others' viewpoints, but remember Lucy and Aslan: sometimes other people can't see the message God has for you.

Your friends may worry if a new direction won't utilize any of your schooling or training. Or they may question whether a relationship can really last. They may be right, but they may simply be too practical! However, if people you trust are especially concerned, be sure you've considered all four guidance systems and the values your decision honors.

In the midst of these tensions, God is still sovereign. This means you may not live with your first choices. However, how often when your plans are stymied do you later learn how disastrous your first choice would have been?

Some people approach God as they might a hassled parent (i.e., if they keep nagging, Mom or Dad will give in out of self-defense). But children with loving, well-rested parents don't always get what they want, because the adults sometimes see a bigger picture and say no. So does God.

God's sovereignty means that if you misread the message of your circumstances, God can redeem your mistakes. You can't go so far in the wrong direction that God can't find you. Further, even if the sins of others bring tragedy, God can redeem it in the fullness of time. Gerald Sittser, who lost his wife, mother, and young daughter in a single auto accident, acknowledges that he never "got over it," but learned to absorb the losses into his life until they became a part of who he is. He says,

> Gifts of grace come to all of us. But we must be ready to see and willing to receive these gifts. It will require a kind of sacrifice, the sacrifice of believing that, however painful our

losses, life can still be good—good in a different way than before, but nevertheless good.[2]

Looking for God in the Dark

Even though it seems at times as if God either isn't interested in our lives or we somehow missed the road markers that told us which way to go, God is with us. While Sittser would do anything to relive the day of the accident so it didn't occur, he also knows that because he chose to deal with his grief and continue on for the sake of his other children, he's learned more about faith, parenting, and maturity than he thought possible. His life will never be as he dreamed but he's learned that it can, in an unexpected way, be good.

So often when people get further down the path and look back at what seemed the bleakest of circumstances, their perspective has changed. They see that God somehow used those circumstances: maybe it was a time of learning, of building a relationship, waiting for the right moment, or leaning on God. Not that God sent the circumstances to teach a lesson, but when those events came to pass, God used evil for good. Their state of affairs is not of their own choosing. It may never compensate for what is lost. But a new life can be built that points to a very different yet favorable future. As Sören Kierkegaard put it, "Life must be understood backward. But then one forgets the other clause—that it must be lived forward."[3]

Living life forward is confusing and scary, but it's our only choice. Consider Joe, the youngest of many brothers and his father's favorite, who planned on taking over his father's agricultural holdings. His cocksure attitude so infuriated his siblings that they actually arranged for him to be kidnapped and taken out of the country. Living virtually as a slave, imprisoned for crimes he didn't commit, the biblical Joseph certainly went

---

2 Gerald Sittser, *A Grace Disguised: How the Soul Grows Through Loss* (Grand Rapids, Mich.: Zondervan Publishing House, 1996), 68.

3 *Journals and Papers* [1843] , vol. I

through much more than mere family dysfunction!

Yes, God used the evil intentions of Joseph's brothers to place him in Egypt, where he would eventually save his family from famine, but the story has more lessons than "God can turn evil into good" for anyone who is struggling to figure out the whys and wherefores of God's guidance.

Perhaps you long for a clear vision of your future, thinking, "If only God would show me the goal, I'd be better able to make the right choices to get there." Joseph is perhaps one of the best examples of how off-target this desire can be. Joseph knew the end from the start, that someday he would be great. However, he never would have gotten there on his own—he angered his entire family, especially his father, by telling them of a dream that implied he would eventually lead his family. This prideful, well-treated, favored Joseph had no incentive to learn anything.

Would Joseph ever have changed if he'd stayed at home? Tending his father's sheep during his young adulthood didn't provide the maturity and management experience he needed to be second-in-command of Egypt. Look at the clear pattern visible in the context of God's ultimate goal for Joseph.

Joseph's first job was as an attendant to Potiphar, captain of Pharaoh's guard. Joseph wasted little time if any on self-pity, for we read, "When his master saw that the Lord was with him and that the Lord gave him success in everything he did, Joseph found favor in his eyes and became his attendant. Potiphar put him in charge of his household, and he entrusted to his care everything he owned" (Genesis 39:3-4). Joseph's new position in this well-to-do home was similar to managing a small business— a far cry from the grazing fields of Canaan and an excellent place to learn about inventory management, planning, and organization.

His complacency, however, was shattered by the overtures of Potiphar's wife. Her lies landed Joseph in the royal dungeon, the site of his second "job." Again, instead of despairing, Joseph looked to God. Soon the warden put him in charge of the other prisoners. Think of the skills in negotiation, decision-making, and persuasion that Joseph practiced as two full years passed!

Joseph also matured. His empathy with other prisoners contrasts markedly with the arrogance he displayed in Canaan; he heard about the dreams of the cupbearer and baker after noting their downcast expressions and inquiring about their sadness. Interpreting their dreams eventually brought Joseph to Pharaoh.

Contrast the Joseph of Canaan—"My sheaf rose and stood upright, while your sheaves gathered around mine and bowed down to it" (Genesis 37:7)—with the Joseph who came before Pharaoh: "I cannot [interpret a dream] but God will give Pharaoh the answer he desires" (Genesis 41:16). The intervening years made Joseph into a humble yet wise and perceptive person. Pharaoh recognized this in just a few moments and Joseph was given his third job as Pharaoh's second-in-command.

God's Timing Is Perfect

However bleak Joseph's circumstances in Egypt had seemed, events had tracked with God's timing. But Joseph had no way of knowing the future as the failure or shortcomings of *other* people pushed him down—his father's favoritism, his brothers' jealousy, the deceit of Potiphar's wife, the cupbearer's forgetfulness. Sound familiar? If one could see no further than those moments, Joseph's future was derailed.

And the bleak years dragged on. Joseph was thirty years old when Pharaoh put him in charge of Egypt; he had been only seventeen when his brothers sold him into slavery. Joseph had thirteen years to wonder why all this had happened to him. The two years in prison after the cupbearer promised to mention him to Pharaoh must have seemed an eternity to Joseph. Yet the months went by—until the moment Pharaoh needed an administrator of Joseph's caliber. God's timing was perfect: into jail in time to hear the dreams of a person close to Pharaoh, out of jail in time to organize the grain supply of the entire country.

Does this mean that we take whatever comes our way with our

hands folded because "it will all work out"? No. It means that like Joseph, whatever comes our way we keep trusting God, believing that God can help us prepare for a future different from our original dream, yet still worth living.

Waiting may be easier if you contemplate that God's hand is on your circumstances. God has a time for everything under the sun and, more importantly, *God is with you, as Joseph experienced, even when you feel beyond hope.* If you continue to trust, looking for the purpose in detours and the positive choices you can make, the doors of the waiting room, like the doors of the Egyptian prison, will eventually swing open. The reasons for those detours—even thirteen-year detours like Joseph experienced—become crystal clear. Like Joseph or Gerald Sittser, you may still wish with all of your being that those events had never happened. But when we face our unchangeable circumstances, God can somehow redeem wrong with a grace we never imagined possible.

Red Light, Green Light?

Because of our broken world and the spiritual warfare that surrounds us, learning from circumstances is seldom black and white, or simple. The idea that if the doors open for you along a certain path God must be with you is not only unbiblical but downright dangerous. Although we haven't taken an official tally, the Bible seems to have more examples of times where circumstances would have misled people than shown them God's will! A few examples:

> Saul took three thousand chosen men from all Israel and set out to look for David and his men near the Crags of the Wild Goats. He came to the sheep pens along the way; a cave was there, and Saul went in to relieve himself. David and his men were far back in the cave. The men said, "This is the day the Lord spoke of when he said to you, 'I will give your enemy into your hands for you to deal with as you wish'" (1 Samuel 24:4).

David didn't kill Saul, but only snipped a corner from the man's robe. Afterward, David begged forgiveness even for this, saying it was wrong to so dishonor a person whom God had anointed. David recognized that what the circumstances seemed to dictate contradicted higher laws: we are not to kill, and we are to respect those whom God has chosen.

> About midnight Paul and Silas were praying and singing hymns to God, and the other prisoners were listening to them. Suddenly there was such a violent earthquake that the foundations of the prison were shaken. At once all the prison doors flew open, and everybody's chains came loose. The jailer woke up, and when he saw the prison doors open, he drew his sword and was about to kill himself because he thought the prisoners had escaped. (Acts 16:25-27)

Wouldn't you have fled? But Paul and Silas stayed put and were able to baptize the jailer and his whole family.

> That evening after sunset the people brought to Jesus all the sick and demon-possessed. The whole town gathered at the door, and Jesus healed many who had various diseases. He also drove out many demons, but he would not let the demons speak because they knew who he was. (Mark 1:32-34)

If the crowds were taking in your message and you were the number-one attraction in town, would you think that God was blessing your ministry and you should remain? But Jesus left Capernaum the very next morning.

With his children dead, his lands in ruins, and his health destroyed, Job looked to his friends for comfort, only to hear them assert that his troubles must be the result of sin in his life:

> You say to God, "My beliefs are flawless and I am pure in your sight." Oh, how I wish that God would speak, that he would open his lips against you and disclose to you the secrets of wisdom, for true wisdom has two sides. Know this: God has even forgotten some of your sin. (Job 11:4-6)

Yet we know from the first chapter of Job that he is without fault; God allowed Satan to test him. Job's circumstances were not the result of his actions.

Thus the number one rule about discerning God's will from circumstances is this:

> Open doors don't *necessarily*
> point to God's will.
>
> Closed doors don't *necessarily*
> mean a certain path isn't God's will.

At this point you may be asking, "What kind of a guidance system is this, anyway? I can't trust any of the instruments!" Yes you can, but the instruments you are trying to read are much deeper than the facts of a situation. You are trying to read what God is telling you in these situations.

Paul speaks frequently of an open door, but let's look at these texts:

> When [Paul and Barnabas] arrived, they called the church together and related all that God had done with them, and how he had opened a door of faith for the Gentiles. (Acts 14:27 NRSV)

> I will stay in Ephesus until Pentecost, for a wide door for effective work has opened to me, and there are many adversaries. (1 Corinthians 16:8-9 NRSV)

> When I came to Troas to proclaim the good news of Christ, a door was opened for me in the Lord; but my mind could not rest because I did not find my brother Titus there. So I said farewell to them and went on to Macedonia. (2 Corinthians 2:12-13 NRSV)

> At the same time pray for us as well that God will open to us a door for the word, that we may declare the mystery of Christ, for which I am in prison. (Colossians 4:3 NRSV)

In these verses, taken together, Paul uses the term "open door" to describe places where people were receptive to Paul's messages. This doesn't mean that preaching the Gospel met no opposition. Paul was stoned and left for dead while opening the "door of faith for the Gentiles" (Acts 14:19). Describing Ephesus, Paul mentions his adversaries in the same breath as the open door. In Troas, Paul left despite an open door. Yes, there was an opportunity for ministry, but Paul weighed his options and decided it was more important to search for Titus, who hadn't arrive as expected in Troas. And in the Colossians passage, Paul, even in prison, is simply looking for another avenue for spreading the Gospel.

There is little evidence, then, in the references to open doors in the Bible, for a "red light, green light" view of finding God's will. Because doing the will of God is so often wholly contrary to the ways of the world, difficulties along the way simply don't mean that you are off course. Sometimes closed doors swing open after phenomenal perseverance. If Moses had been looking for open doors, would he have gone back to Pharaoh ten times? Would Paul have gone back on the ocean after being shipwrecked twice, or would he have considered preaching closer to home? On Easter morning, would the women who had followed Jesus have dared to go to his tomb with the Roman guards all around it, or would they have stayed away?

True Circumstantial Evidence

So where are circumstances used as guidance in the Bible? By people who were already in a relationship with God, who were open to learning new things about God or themselves from their situations, who stood ready to bless God in all circumstances, and who weren't blinded by their own notions of the way things should go. They knew that God might just as easily require a hard task as show them a smooth path.

Ruth, the young woman who was so faithful to her mother-in-law, Naomi, went to gather grain for the two of them. Custom dictated that widows could work behind harvesters, gleaning what they dropped. Ruth didn't know who owned the field she was working in; she just happened to pick the field of Boaz, one of Naomi's relatives. Naomi helped her act on this fortuitous circumstance and Ruth became Boaz's wife (see the book of Ruth).

The Pharaoh of Egypt had declared that all Hebrew baby boys be killed. Moses' mother tried to avoid this fate by putting her son in a basket, which her daughter Miriam set afloat in the Nile River. The basket floated right into the hands of the princess of Egypt. When the princess saw the baby crying, Miriam said, "Shall I fetch a Hebrew woman to be its wet nurse?" Thus Moses was nursed by his own mother (see Exodus 2).

The young Jewish woman Esther must have wondered how and why she became queen of Persia. However, when a conspiracy arose to have all of the Jews killed, Esther's uncle said, "Who knows? Perhaps you have come to royal dignity for just such a time as this" (Esther 4:14 NRSV).

In these cases, people acted on the incredible circumstances they saw in front of them—yet with no assurance of success. Ruth didn't know she'd get to be Boaz's wife. Miriam didn't know whether Moses would be saved or killed. Esther didn't know what would happen when she entered the throne room uninvited. They took risks after they weighed their circumstances against what they already knew about God, which brings us to the second rule of seeing God in circumstances:

You have to trust God before you can make the most of your circumstances.

Perhaps you remember the movie The Karate Kid. Deep down, Daniel, the young karate student, doesn't really trust the old master. He can't understand why the old man makes him paint fences, moving the brush up and down, up and down, for hours. Or wash half a dozen antique cars with his right hand and wax them with his left. Or sand endless wooden walkways with steady circular motions. Finally, Daniel has had enough; he signed on to learn karate, not to fix up old stuff. But the old master shows him that these chores trained his muscles, ingraining all the basic moves of karate.

Because Joseph trusted God, the house of Potiphar and the Pharaoh's dungeon could be training grounds for him. Instead of groaning, "Why me?" Joseph continued to believe that God was with him in spite of his circumstances, and the training he therefore received in those places was vital to his eventual role as second-in-command of all of Egypt.

Trust God. This doesn't mean trust everyone else you come into contact with, but trust that no matter what your situation, God can somehow use it. Even more importantly, trust that God is with you. Part of trusting God is acknowledging that your Creator knows more than you do about what will bring fulfillment in your life. Only then can you step out with confidence no matter what the circumstances.

Look at Caleb and the other spies who traveled into Canaan to learn about the military might of its people. Most of the spies looked at the circumstances—fortified cities and strong armies—and said, "No way!" Caleb said, "If God wants us to have this land, we will be able to take it" (Numbers 14:8, authors' paraphrase). Caleb looked past the circumstances because he remembered what God had already told them directly: the land would be theirs. He knew the third rule.

> Your circumstances are just one
> of the four guidance systems.

Living by circumstances alone leaves us vulnerable to "red light, green light" thinking: we all too easily make the mistake of thinking that a smooth path means we're in God's will and a rough path means somewhere we missed a turn. However, it's essential to check against the other guidance systems what you think a situation means.

What you see in circumstances won't contradict what you know from the Bible. For example:

- No matter how wonderful the first date seemed, we aren't to marry people who haven't asked God to be Lord of their lives.
- We aren't wise to accept any accusation against an elder, no matter what the circumstances might seem to prove, except on the evidence of two or three witnesses.
- We are to take out the logs from our own eyes before removing a speck from someone else's, no matter how much trouble they're causing.
- We are to be honest in our own business dealings even if we're forced to deal with a swindler. A just end won't justify shady means.

It may also take all four guidance systems to fill us in on exactly what we're supposed to do in a situation. For example, in the story of Philip and the eunuch, the Holy Spirit led Philip directly to the eunuch's chariot. Once there, Philip knew to use his gift of evangelism. He helped the Ethiopian understand what Scripture had to say about Jesus. Then the eunuch employed the fourth guidance system—circumstances—saying, "Look, here is water. Why shouldn't I be baptized?" Remember, they were on the sixty-plus-mile desert road between Jerusalem and Gaza, where there are few streams suitable for a New Testament-style baptismal soaking. The eunuch took advantage of a coincidence. (See Acts 8:26-39.)

On the other hand, too often we let our circumstances guide us without even evaluating them. For example, how many people drift into marrying the person they're dating their senior year of high school or college? Or become a teacher because one of their parents was a teacher? Or stay on a single career path because once upon a time someone offered him or her a job in that field? Circumstances shouldn't dictate your next step without careful evaluation through the other guidance systems.

One of David's friends, a great science student, went through a logical analysis of his skills and career prospects to choose dentistry. He excelled on the dental boards and was easily accepted into dental school—but he didn't visit a dentist's office until the end of his senior year. Within three hours he knew he'd hate being a dentist. All of those open doors hadn't pointed to a career in dentistry after all.

Or, we can let one aspect of a decision overwhelm other factors. Many people are especially vulnerable to giving financial factors too much weight. One of Jane's friends told her boss that she was quitting her job as an office manager to stay home with her three children. He quickly offered her a 30 percent raise. She almost changed her mind—until Jane pulled out some statistics that showed he'd been *underpaying* her by more than that for years.

If money is a major factor, look back at *all* of your values. Are you interpreting money as a "green light" from God, who warns us against storing up treasures on earth? Most of us err on one side or the other of this issue: we are either too pragmatic or too altruistic. Consider what happens in many home-buying situations. When a couple finally has the means to purchase a bigger home and finds a place they like, they read the signs as approval from God—without considering how that big, new home might get in the way of values like family-togetherness (there are now so many separate rooms that family members are encouraged to pursue their interests on their own), simplicity (the home locks them into a mortgage-run lifestyle), or even a lack of reality (they have to furnish the house as lavishly as their new neighbors furnish theirs, forgetting how little most people of the world possess).

However, sometimes we can be so convinced of what seems right because of our values or passions that we aren't open to what the circumstances are saying. There is tension between the importance of identifying your values and passions at a particular point in time and being willing, as your situation changes, to forgo those very same passions you believed were from God.

> Until you hold lightly to your own hopes
> and plans, you can't hear what God is
> saying through circumstances.

God is sovereign, which means we aren't in charge. And that's good, because we don't know as much as God does. As we said at the start, the word "Lord" has no content unless you sometimes go directions you wouldn't choose on your own. Some of those directions will require difficult tasks or stands, but they will still be better than your first choice, even if you can't see that at the outset.

If you're speaking, you can't hear God. If you're sure that you know where you're supposed to end up, you may not be receptive to the course changes God is trying to make. One college student, for example, fell head-over-heels in love with a graduate student. He was funny, full of great ideas for their time together, and seemed to love her for who she was. They agreed within five days of their first meeting that they were meant for each other and became secretly engaged. The woman was so certain that this was the right relationship that she ignored:

- the opinions of her friends, who thought he loved himself more than her
- her parents, who distrusted him from their first meeting (her father unconsciously stabbed his steak knife into a table when she hinted that they might be getting serious)
- her fiancé's temper, which suggested his total inability to make a permanent commitment
- his plans for moving right after the wedding, which would keep her from finishing her degree.

It took nine months and a major fight (thankfully a nonviolent one) before she broke off the engagement (and yes, she is now happily married to a wonderful man). Yet how much sooner might she have seen the problems in the first relationship if she hadn't closed herself off from reevaluating it?

In some areas of life, we expect to hear a no on the way to a yes. Few people, for example, expect to land a job the first time they ever go for an interview. Yet if the no's pile up, we begin wondering if we are pursuing the wrong opportunities. Maybe so, but maybe the right one is still waiting. We can't see it, but God is aware of what it will be.

Remember the story of the resurrection of Lazarus? His sisters, Mary and Martha, waited four days after his death for Jesus to come. Surely they had given up hope that God was going to heal their brother. But the "yes" they finally saw was far more miraculous than an earlier healing would have been.

> About three years into my financial career, I wanted to change employers. I had a great first interview with the chief financial officer of a multinational company and was invited for a full day of interviews. The morning went well, but I faltered in a couple of the afternoon sessions and was not offered a job.
>
> However, when the head of my department heard that I'd been looking for another job, he promoted me and transferred me to another area that was a perfect match for my skills. I couldn't have found a better fit anywhere. And not too long after, I learned more about the other company—I wouldn't have meshed at all well with their values.
>
> The moral isn't "Spread the word that you're searching so you'll get promoted" but "Even if you're unhappy in a certain spot, the answer may not be the obvious one—leaving—but something even better that God is orchestrating."
>
> —Jane

In essence, hold lightly to dreams. They can be inspiring, they can be motivating, but they may also be the product of your own desires, not God's. Name dreams as dreams, call expectations what they are. There may be many detours—if you think you're supposed to be headed a certain way, you may feel betrayed rather than delayed.

One of the ways to make sure you are holding dreams lightly is to use what many Christians refer to as the prayer of relinquishment. In effect, say, "Okay God, I don't understand what you're doing here. I thought for certain you wanted me to be well/be a dentist/get married, but I turn it all over to you and relinquish my control over the situation."

Robert Walker, who served as editor of several Christian magazines, was certain that he was cut out to be a writer and pursued training at every opportunity. After many initial successes, he couldn't sell an article and wondered whether he was writing for money or for God:

> Squarely I faced the possibility that God might want me to be a preacher or a missionary or an evangelist—even though I could scarcely see how I had any talents in those directions. In desperation that night, I cried out to the Lord, "Give me a call. Let me know plainly what you want me to do and no matter what it is or where I must go, I am yours for whatever purpose you wish."
>
> [Soon] I realized that God did not want or need my talents. What he wanted was me.[4]

Walker went on to be a writer, but only after he relinquished his *right* to be a writer could God assure him that this indeed was his calling. Realizing this freed him from the burden of wondering about his motivations and allowed him to dedicate his writing to God.

At times, you may never understand why your plans aren't God's plans. Instead, God may use an event simply to assure you that you are loved.

> *My husband and I couldn't have been any more fiscally responsible about the small home we had built, mostly with our own hands, for our growing family. But when it was completed, the company that had guaranteed our mortgage looked at the final paperwork. Same numbers, same reviewers, but a new answer: No.*

---

4 John Sigsworth, compiler, *How I Found God's Will for My Life* (Grand Rapids, Mich.: Zondervan Publishing House, 1960), 61-62.

Credit was very tight at the time and one bank after another refused our loan requests. In church that Sunday, aware that we would probably lose our house in a few days, I couldn't bring myself to sing the praise songs with the words "I believe." Did I?

Could I believe in a God who seemingly let us fall?

Tears filled my eyes as I admitted I couldn't join the singing. I opened my eyes as the song ended and looked down on the seat in front of me. There it was, clear and distinct on the royal blue upholstered chair—a tiny, round seed. Just one. Like one I'd had as a child in a glass-bubble necklace. A mustard seed.

The verse came to me, "If you have faith the size of a mustard seed..." and I knew I could believe just that much. I left church that day with a seed of hope planted in my heart.

—Tanya, 45, editor

> Sometimes God is trying to change
> who you are, not tell you where to go.

A major function of God's guidance is to show us how to be holy people so our lives reflect Jesus. Perhaps Robert Walker needed to struggle until he understood at a higher level why he was gifted as a writer.

Or think back to Joseph. God pinpointed Joseph's developmental needs much more clearly than Joseph could ever do on his own. God is gentle about revealing our weaknesses, or we would soon grow discouraged at our lack of completeness. Yet God provides situations for our growth.

No one would choose to be enslaved and imprisoned to develop the skills they need for the future, yet Joseph must have recalled those experiences with awe at how they had prepared him for his crucial role in the famine years. In times of transition, looking beyond the fears and the hurts requires great effort. However, recognizing God's economies—how God puts all of our experiences to work—can provide hope.

We don't think God sends circumstances as punishment—we can't imagine a God who would take the life of a child or orchestrate tragedies simply to teach someone else a spiritual lesson! However, when tragedies strike in this broken world, God can use whatever circumstances we are in to develop our character:

> In Christ we have also obtained an inheritance, having been destined according to the purpose of him who accomplishes all things according to his counsel and will, so that we, who were the first to set our hope on Christ, might live for the praise of his glory. (Ephesians 1:11-12 NRSV)

God is as concerned that our lives reflect the Lord's glory as with whether we accomplish good works. If we're becoming holy people as defined by Jesus, the good works will follow. But holiness doesn't necessarily follow good works. Holiness comes from doing the good works God has in mind for us with an attitude that evidences the fruit of the spirit.

Some of our everyday struggles are simply in our best interest. We joke about "Be careful what you pray for—you just may get it!" Ask for patience—and you just may be tortured by the slowest bank teller ever. Ask for joy—and you may be forced to find the humor in finding your toddler spreading the pumpkin pie he pulled off the counter all over himself and the carpet. Ask for peace—and you may end up arbitrating a neighborhood spat so a longer truce may endure. Unfortunately, we seldom develop character when circumstances are good. People who deal best with sudden fame had their values firmly in place before wealth or recognition came their way.

God may take advantage of circumstances in other ways. Are you supposed to learn from a person who's been placed beside you? Have you ever taken on one too many commitments, only to find that the most burdensome allowed you to meet someone who became an important friend? Or been encouraged to take on a project, only to find out that it was bigger and more central to what someone needed than you could ever imagine?

During our Secret Pals exchange at school, I picked out a card for the new teacher whose name I'd drawn. The card I chose had some of my favorite storybook characters on it and a verse about not having to be alone. I thought it would help my new colleague to know she was a part of a team. I actually signed it from all of the teachers, saying to knock on any door for help any time.

All year long it remained on her desk, and I thought, How nice, she must have liked it. *At the very end of the year when we were cleaning out desks, I asked her if she knew who had sent the card. She went white when I asked her but said, "No."*

"I did. Did you like it?"

"It was very precious to me. I gave one just like it to my fiancé in the hospital shortly before he died last year."

God worked through me much more directly than I could have if I'd analyzed how to reach out to her!

—Rachel, 40, teacher

Maybe you're in a situation where you can develop a certain skill or gift (or maybe the poor choices of others have placed you in a bad situation, but God can still bring good out of it). Daniel was hand-picked to enter the king's service in Babylon and thus received three years of education in language and literature, which placed him in a position where he could influence the king. Joseph, too, developed skills, first as a slave in Potiphar's house, then as a prisoner in the Pharaoh's dungeon. Daniel and Joseph believed God was still with them, which allowed God to work through them in any circumstance. Jane learned to revise her writing as a junior staffer at the Federal Reserve when a committee of twelve "tore apart" the speeches she wrote for senior officers. Being forced to take criticism quietly was great preparation for coauthoring, however torturous at the time.

Perhaps by now you're saying, "No, my circumstances are my own fault. I'm stuck with them because of what I did. Therefore, I can't expect God to do anything about them." Hear this: *The dynamic will of God is reshaping your life all the time, already factoring in your brokenness.* The sovereign will of God is bigger than any mistake you might have made, any dysfunctional family situation, any corrupt system. God has many ways of redeeming both your failures and the seemingly defeating ways of the enemy. If you doubt this, reread the Bible stories of David and Bathsheba, the woman at the well, Saul of Tarsus, Jacob and Esau—the list is endless.

And you can't stray so far that the Holy Spirit can't find you:

> If I go up to the heavens, you are there;
>   if I make my bed in the depths, you are there.
> If I rise on the wings of the dawn,
>   if I settle on the far side of the sea,
> even there your hand will guide me,
>   your right hand will hold me fast.
> (Psalm 139:8-10)

God is with you, no matter how much or how little of your current situation is of your own doing. You simply may not be able to see how everything will work out.

> God uses circumstances as
> a lamp unto our feet
> rather than a lighthouse
> beaming far into the future.

In Psalm 119:105 we read, "Your word is a lamp to my feet and a light for my path." That doesn't mean we can see clearly what is ahead. Take a closer look at the imagery in this verse.

1. If you're using a lamp, that means it's dark out. You're having trouble seeing where to go.

2. The light referred to was an unsteady, flickering wick in a little vessel of oil, not a search party flashlight.

3. The light from this little lamp would let you see clearly to take your next footstep safely, not to run ahead quickly.

4. The light doesn't take away the darkness—you might consider the darkness your doubts, the evil around us, or the difficulties of uncertainty—but it does allow us to keep moving in spite of our being surrounded by darkness.

We can see ahead clearly one step at a time. And while at times it would be nice to see further into the future, Jesus tells us, "Therefore do not worry about tomorrow, for tomorrow will worry about itself. Each day has enough trouble of its own" (Matthew 6:34). God can only let us see so far ahead—or we'll either quit moving in an effort to avoid inevitable bumps in this life or we'll quit trying because we think we've got it all figured out.

> *Although we'd known by the seventh month of my pregnancy that there was something seriously wrong with our third child, we also knew that we couldn't predict what would happen. So little Sammy was born, heart defect and all. We rocked him, hugged him, and did everything we could to help him feel loved. Someone had given him a little music box that played "Edelweiss," and we played it so many times that the handle broke and my husband tossed it aside. On the sixth day of Sammy's life, he died in my arms. As the nurse lovingly took his body from me, the music box spontaneously started to play again. It was as if God were saying, "Go ahead and grieve for Sam, but the music will sound again in your lives."*
>
> —Kit, 39, teacher

This guidance system is often about waiting—as did Paul, who spent about nine years in Tarsus after his conversion before starting his great missions. Or Jacob, who labored fourteen years for a wife.

> *When I first worked on my small group ministry materials, I'd had significant encouragement from someone who seemed ready to publish them. I did an extensive amount of primary*

research into different methods, reviewed stacks of literature on what was working with different small group models, and finally developed what I thought was a sound improvement in small group leadership. When I presented my ideas, I found out that the publisher had already chosen a different model. After some soul-searching, I set aside the project.

Four years later, during a luncheon, another pastor casually asked me, "Do you know anything about small group leadership?" His and fourteen other churches were having difficulties with the very model my materials had been written to overturn. I couldn't have asked for a better platform for my resources than this one that God had obviously prepared.

As I worked toward publishing my small group manuals in this new environment, I saw how I would have lost control of what I wanted to do if the first opportunity had come to fruition.

—David

Waiting can also be a product of the roles you've already agreed to play or are assigned as part of your stage in life. For example, pastors (or people in any line of work) who have also chosen to be spouses and parents must balance those roles against their calling as a minister (or their particular job and ambitions). Their spouses expect—and deserve—that they will abide by the commitments those choices entailed. Biblically, Jesus told us that we may need to turn our backs on our families (Matthew 12:48-50), but in view of Paul's instructions to Titus about elders and deacons needing to effectively lead their families (Titus 1:6), a better way to interpret Jesus' statement might be that we can't let their beliefs keep us from holding true to our beliefs. This is an example of taking account of the whole of Scripture before interpreting what the Bible has to say on a topic.

Finally, since we can only see a limited distance ahead, even if we're in the same circumstances twice, we need to seek God's guidance as to what to do. King David was well aware of how his success in battle depended on his listening to God:

Now the Philistines had come and spread out in the Valley of Rephaim; so David inquired of the Lord, "Shall I go and attack the Philistines? Will you hand them over to me?" The Lord answered him, "Go, for I will surely hand the Philistines over to you." So David went to Baal Perazim, and there he defeated them....

Once more the Philistines came up and spread out in the Valley of Rephaim; so David inquired of the Lord, and he answered, "Do not go straight up, but circle around behind them and attack them in front of the balsam trees. As soon as you hear the sound of marching in the tops of the balsam trees, move quickly, because that will mean the Lord has gone out in front of you to strike the Philistine army." So David did as the Lord commanded him, and he struck down the Philistines all the way from Gibeon to Gezer. (2 Samuel 5:18-20, 22-25)

David knew that God guided him only one step at a time. He went back to the source of strength and wisdom before going into battle again, even on the same battlefield. Perhaps David couldn't control the course of a battle, but he could control whether his army used God's plan of attack.

> Part of discerning God's will in difficult circumstances is determining what you can and cannot change.

God is aware of every detail of your circumstances, down to the hairs on your head. But that doesn't lessen the need for prayer. Is this a time for action or a time for waiting? Are there lessons to learn? Perhaps you need insight into why or how these circumstances came about or the roles you might play. And perhaps most important, what can you change? Prayer often does change things, but the biggest thing that changes is you and the input you seek.

My eldest daughter's health problems required frequent doctor visits and she resented every one of them. Tired of the struggle, I prayed that the next visit would go smoothly. Instead, Kelly went crazy to the point that we had to chase her around the office to give her a simple immunization shot. To make matters worse, we had the office's least sympathetic nurse, whose lecturing simply compounded the problem.

As I prayed about what had gone wrong, I got a different answer from God than I had expected. "Your daughter wants to be treated like an adult. Be totally honest with her about what is to come, let her make choices when possible, and tell her the truth when there are no choices." My husband and I set new goals to ensure that Kelly didn't become afraid of seeking medical treatment. We couldn't magically change our daughter's attitude, but we could change our attitude toward her. We recognized that it would take time to undo her frustrations with her health care, feelings developed over several years.

—Corinne, 46, attorney

> Sometimes our circumstances are
> because of choices we've already made.

While this family worked through their daughter's medical treatments, the parents sought their daughter's forgiveness for not being more sensitive sooner. Situations don't always improve immediately. Sometimes we need to repent or ask forgiveness. And even then, sometimes we have to live with the consequences of our actions.

Jonah never would have been cast overboard in the midst of a storm if he'd gone to Nineveh when God first asked him to. Being in the belly of a whale may have convinced Jonah that he should obey God and act as a prophet to Nineveh, but he was there because he tried to do his own will instead of God's.

And Jonah was lucky. The consequences of his actions affected only him. God calmed the storm, and the others on the boat with him were safe. The people of Nineveh got the message they needed. We obviously aren't always so lucky. Our choices may be irreversible. They may have hurt not only ourselves but others as well.

If we find ourselves in these situations, we have lots of company:

- God *forgave* King David, but there were still terrible consequences from his affair with Bathsheba, beginning with the death of the child they had conceived.
- God *forgave* Moses for smacking a rock to get water rather than wait for it to be provided, but didn't let him enter the Promised Land.
- Nixon may have been pardoned for his part in Watergate, but he wasn't reinstated as president.

After dealing with our first attitudes of shock and grief, finding God's guidance in such circumstances requires repentance, turning to God to ask, "Okay I'm here, what am I to learn?" Not "God sent this as punishment" but "How am I responsible for what has happened to me and how can I prevent a repeat?"

Samson is an example of what might happen if you fail to learn from your circumstances. He was supposed to keep to himself the secret of his great strength, but he was so infatuated with Delilah that he failed to learn from her treachery.

The Philistines had bribed Delilah to find out the secret of Samson's strength. When she asked him the first time, he lied to her, saying, "Tie me up with seven bowstrings that haven't been dried." Delilah did it while the Philistines hid, ready to capture him. Of course Samson was able to immediately break the thongs.

After that experience, would you have a thread of trust in Delilah? Yet when she asked again about the source of his strength, Samson said, "Weave my hair into the fabric on a loom." She did, setting the Philistines on him again, but of course he escaped.

Samson still stayed with Delilah, listening to such nonsense as:

> "How can you say, 'I love you,' when you won't confide in me? This is the third time you have made a fool of me and

haven't told me the secret of your great strength." With such nagging she prodded him day after day until he was tired to death. So he told her everything. "No razor has ever been used on my head," he said, "because I have been a Nazirite set apart to God since birth. If my head were shaved, my strength would leave me, and I would become as weak as any other man." When Delilah saw that he had told her everything, she sent word to the rulers of the Philistines, "Come back once more; he has told me everything." So the rulers of the Philistines returned with the silver [for Delilah] in their hands. Having put him to sleep on her lap, she called a man to shave off the seven braids of his hair, and so began to subdue him. And his strength left him. (Judges 16:15-19)

What do you think was on Samson's mind after the Philistines blinded him and forced him to toil at a grindstone in prison? Paying attention to circumstances can help us learn our lesson the first time and avoid a cruel messenger.

How Do We Tap This Guidance System?

God wants to give us input to our circumstances, but we have to be receptive. We have to know ourselves, know the Bible, know the Holy Spirit. That's why we put this system last.

1. **The first hint for understanding circumstances is to ask God what is going on.** "If any of you is lacking in wisdom, ask God, who gives to all generously and ungrudgingly, and it will be given you" (James 1:5 NRSV).
    Talk out loud with God. Pray,
        This is what I see around me.
        This is what I'm feeling about it.
        This is what I can add from the Bible.
        When I put it all together,
            this is the best I can do.
        I know I lack wisdom; I'm asking for your help in
            evaluating this situation.
        If you've got another take on it, fill me in quick!

2. Remember that you are part of the body of Christ. You don't have to try to understand everything by yourself. Ask for counsel from wise people. How do they view your circumstances?

3. Use the other guidance systems. That means that after we check what we are seeing against the other guidance systems, we can trust confirmation from our circumstances.

4. Be open to direction for the choices you are facing. Part of Jesus' message is "I have come that they may have life, and have it to the full" (John 10:10). God has our welfare in mind—if you really like one potential boss and distrust another, consider that God is perhaps at work. If you're looking at two jobs that are equal in terms of pay and advancement, all other things being equal, take the one that seems to have the atmosphere most suited for you. This is why understanding God's wisdom and our own design must precede looking for guidance from the circumstances around us.

5. Worry less if you know that your actions will further God's work. If a decision on your part clearly fosters justice or love and is consistent with Scripture, etc., can you really be out of God's will?

Let circumstances be a light to your path, not a shadow that clouds your vantage point of what God might be saying. If it's really too dark to see—all paths seem equally good or questionable—switch guidance systems. What do the Scriptures, your special design, and the Holy Spirit have to say? Just as birds can fly at night, relying on other systems, you can continue on whether or not a door swings open right in front of you to show you which way to go.

When the weight of decision burdens my soul
and I struggle to hear you,
I want you to take me by the hand.
My will so often blinds me to your will.

  Yet,
      at each dead end,
      I find that you came with me,
      ready to guide me as I try to put back the pieces my
          mistakes broke loose.

As I remember those dead ends,
the tenderness with which you turned me around
envelops me and guides me
  as I once again ponder,
      "Which way, God?"

  This time, help me to see you. Amen.

Reflections for Your Own LifeDirections

1. Look through our main points in this chapter. Which ones caught your attention the most? Why?
   - Sometimes it isn't the facts of a situation that matter, but what God is trying to teach you or draw to your attention.
   - Because the message is deeper than the facts, neither open nor closed doors are enough evidence for a decision.
   - Adverse circumstances don't mean you're out of God's will.
   - Favorable circumstances don't necessarily mean you've found God's will.
   - Circumstances are often about changing who we are.
   - Circumstances may only light the next step of our journey. We still may not have a clear vision of the final destination.

2. When have you interpreted circumstances as an open door, only to find out later that you made a poor choice? What other method God uses to guide us might have helped you choose more wisely?

3. Looking back to the life decision you recorded at the end of chapter 1, did you over- or under-emphasize this system? Were there things you dismissed as "coincidence" that perhaps were more important than you acknowledged?

4. Check the texts on open doors (pages 139–140). For Paul, an open door was a place receptive to the Gospel. If you have a mission statement, what would indicate an open door for you, despite struggles or opposition?

5. On pages 146–147 we discuss the prayer of relinquishment. What might you need to relinquish before God can guide you? A particular career? Your desire to be married? To have children? To reach a certain standard of living?

6. On pages 138–139, read again how Job knew his circumstances were not the result of any wrongdoings on his part. Are you carrying any false burdens, taking the blame for circumstances that aren't your fault?

Experiencing God's Guidance Through Circumstances

At the end of each chapter that describes one of God's four guidance systems is a page, much like this one, to help you apply the system to a specific decision in your life. Appendix C also contains a complete set of these pages, which you may copy for other decisions, as well as a sample summary page to aid you in integrating the information you gain from all of the systems.

For this situation, for this decision, or for today, God seems to be providing me with direct guidance through my circumstances in the following ways:

The Evidence

The facts of my situation	Does this indicate an open door? How?	Does this indicate a closed door? How?

The Interpretation: As I pray about this situation, are the facts the only message? What is God trying to say to me through them?

Am I dismissing anything as a simple coincidence that may be a bigger message from God?

As I share this story with others, what other interpretations do they make?

Are all of these choices within God's will? Is God telling me that any choice is fine?

The Standard: Am I making any decisions or taking as guidance anything that contradicts the wisdom and timeless standards of the Bible?

Chapter 6

All Systems Go!
Integrating the Four Guidance Systems

My child, if you accept my words…
inclining your heart to understanding;
if you indeed cry out for insight…
if you seek it like silver, and search for it as for hidden treasures—
then you will…find the knowledge of God.

—Proverbs 2:1-5 NRSV

Because homing pigeons can't reason, they can't detect whether their guidance systems have been tampered with. On a cloudy day, place a magnetic coil on the head of a pigeon, and two systems are useless—no sun, no sense of direction from the earth's poles. Add a blindfold and you'll have to carry the pigeon to its roost even if it's only a few inches away. The pigeon cannot understand when or why a system is or isn't working.

Fortunately for the pigeon, only a few knowledge-seeking scientists sabotage their ability to navigate. Under normal circumstances their guidance systems compensate for each other and they can keep on their way night or day, rain or shine. But because our decisions are so much more complex, we need a better understanding of how to synthesize the four ways in which God guides us.

In every chapter we've emphasized that these four guidance systems work together. At times you may need only one to know exactly what God wants of you. At other times you may need to look to all four systems. For many reasons, just one system may not be enough:

- We simply don't "see" clearly. Our own plans or blind spots can keep us from seeing what God has in mind.
- The systems fulfill different roles. For example, for many decisions, the Bible may give you general principles but not specifics.
- For the big decisions, more than one system can provide confirmation or a check on rushing to make up our mind.

Joseph, the earthly father of Jesus, illustrates why we need to pay attention to the other systems—even if the answer from one source is crystal clear. Circumstances told Joseph that Mary was pregnant. Scripture gave him the full right to denounce her in public, thus divorcing her and leveling charges that could result in her being stoned to death. The Bible, however, tells us that Joseph was a righteous man—he looked to his values, part of his special design—and decided to divorce her quietly. Of course, an angel appeared in a dream, providing direct guidance of the Spirit to Joseph that Mary was carrying the Son of God.

As you face major decisions, check whether you're disregarding one of the four systems. Ask yourself, "Am I oversimplifying this decision? Are my blind spots ruling this decision? Or are the systems I'm using providing enough guidance?" Again, less significant decisions such as where to go on vacation probably require fewer systems (unless you're debating whether to empty your bank account for a round-the-world cruise).

Remember old King Saul? God said that after the Holy Spirit came upon him, he would be "changed into a different person. After these signs take place, do whatever you think is best, for God will be with you" (1 Samuel 10:6-7 NLT). For people who sincerely seek God's influence for decisions, then—people who have surrendered the lordship of their life—the Holy Spirit can constantly influence their viewpoint on what is best. If you are listening for what God has to say to you and you've studied Scripture and your special design and are open to other forms of guidance when God deems them appropriate, you can be trusted with a vast part of life.

We have presented the systems in the order we have for good

reason. The Bible comes first because its study is a lifelong endeavor, not just a tool for decisions. You alone determine the depth of your foundation of biblical principles, and you can work at this guidance system continually. Similarly, you yourself control how well you understand the second guidance system—your own design, values, and passions. It depends on you—not on any special circumstances or revelation, but on your paying attention to what you've already been given.

The other two systems are not under your control, although the more you understand how they work, the easier it will be for God to use them to guide you. From circumstances and direct leadings of the Holy Spirit you'll receive not only general principles or insights but often more specific information on how to act on those principles, use your gifts, or change directions.

Thus, if we had to give you "rules" for using these guidance systems we might say,

1. Get as familiar as you can with the first two guidance systems—Scripture and your God-given special design. Find some method of Bible study that works for you. Do it in community with others to unearth the blind spots in how you interpret Scripture. And, give yourself the gift of time to work through *LifeKeys* or a similar process until you can rejoice in how God designed you.

2. As you face a specific decision, keep open to direct leadings, but keep moving whether the Holy Spirit communicates with you or not. Remember, the Holy Spirit is already inside of you, influencing your thoughts and ideas. That may be all the guidance you need. God may know that you can be trusted with the rest.

3. Evaluate your circumstances based on the principles in chapter 5. What might God be trying to say to you through what is happening around you?

4. Trust how you are created. Do you tend to rush headlong
into anything or be overcautious? If you want more facts,
more options, better logic, or the opinions of others, take
some time to satisfy those needs. Check though the strengths
and snares for each psychological preference on pages 82–83.
Your personality can make you vulnerable to being too pragmatic or idealistic, selfish or codependent, hurried or hesitant
in this situation. But watch yourself—are you simply trying to
avoid making a decision or actually seeking answers to the questions that trouble you most? You may have to start moving before
God can affirm your choice.

**5. Alone or with someone else, work through what your
particular blind spots or vulnerabilities might be in this decision.** Are you recovering from some loss that might keep you
from seeing reality clearly? Have you had a lot of success with
this type of decision, or so many failures that you second-
guess yourself too readily?

**6. Pray constantly for God's guidance, heart, and wisdom,
acknowledging the Lord in all your circumstances.** Take
enough time for God to speak to you. One way to interpret Paul's
command to pray without ceasing is that God wants to hear from
us all the time, not just when we face a crisis. We are to be
communicating at all times.

If you've determined which options honor God, have gone
through the other steps and still aren't certain, God may be saying, "Go ahead, you can do it. You can't really go out of my will
on this. Enjoy!" God cares deeply about every aspect of your
life, but grants you the assurance not to worry about every little
thing. Do your best to understand the first two guidance systems,
stay open to the others, and be confident that you are operating
within the will of God. "If you hold to my teaching, you are really
my disciples. Then you will know the truth, and the truth will set
you free" (John 8:31-32). Take advantage of that freedom—the
freedom to live without every step being dictated to you!

And one of two things will happen. Either you'll look back a while later and say, "Even though there have been some bumps, I know I walked with God" or you'll turn around and say, "Guess it's time to change direction again, but thanks, God, for sticking with me the whole time." It may be months or even years before you know whether you really made a wrong choice or simply took a detour to gain a new skill or understanding. So don't agonize over it. Just keep looking for God and you'll still be in the right race.

Let's take a look at a few people who managed to keep moving with God. These are not saints but folks who took to heart the words of Isaiah: "'For I know the plans I have for you,' declares the Lord, 'plans to prosper you and not to harm you, plans to give you hope and a future'" (Jeremiah 29:11).

On the Move With No Known Destination

As you read these cases, we'll be asking you to second-guess their decisions and evaluate how your needs, strengths, and doubts differ from theirs. However, we know (because time has passed) that they all walked with God. They made choices that have allowed them to bear fruit in many areas of their lives.

> *Perhaps you've confirmed and affirmed your mission, but can't figure out how to get started or where to go. Or you began with flying colors and things have suddenly dried up. Or you want more information on what to do. If these are your gifts and passions, where specifically can you use them? What job or service opportunity?*

Actually, our first example was a saint. You may have begun to think from all our examples that Paul was on autopilot, with God pulling the strings to tell him which way to turn next, what to say and write, and to determine what would happen to him. But a close look at what we now call his second missionary journey (Acts 15-18) gives a very different picture.

Some time later Paul said to Barnabas, "Let us go back and visit the brothers in all the towns where we preached the word of the Lord and see how they are doing...." Paul chose Silas and left, commended by the brothers to the grace of the Lord. He went through Syria and Cilicia, strengthening the churches.

He came to Derbe and then to Lystra, where a disciple named Timothy lived, whose mother was a Jewess and a believer, but whose father was a Greek. The brothers at Lystra and Iconium spoke well of him. Paul wanted to take him along on the journey, so he circumcised him because of the Jews who lived in that area, for they all knew that his father was a Greek. As they traveled from town to town, they delivered the decisions reached by the apostles and elders in Jerusalem for the people to obey. So the churches were strengthened in the faith and grew daily in numbers.

Paul and his companions traveled throughout the region of Phrygia and Galatia, having been kept by the Holy Spirit from preaching the word in the province of Asia. When they came to the border of Mysia, they tried to enter Bithynia, but the Spirit of Jesus would not allow them to. So they passed by Mysia and went down to Troas. During the night Paul had a vision of a man of Macedonia standing and begging him, "Come over to Macedonia and help us." After Paul had seen the vision, we got ready at once to leave for Macedonia, concluding that God had called us to preach the gospel to them. (Acts 15:36, 40-16:10)

These few paragraphs actually represent a land journey of around one thousand miles, from Jerusalem to Troas—that's like walking from Minneapolis to Houston—and then a few hundred more miles by boat across the Mediterranean. Most of the way, there is no mention of direct leadings by the Holy Spirit, so how did Paul know where to go?

Paul knew his mission and knew that it was based soundly on Scripture. Not only had he worked out his theology as apostle to the Gentiles, but the Council of Jerusalem had agreed with him and blessed his ministry. They referred to such passages as:

> ...that the remnant of men may seek the Lord, and all the Gentiles who bear my name. (In Acts 15:17, James quotes from Amos 9:11-12)

Further, when Paul was converted on the Road to Damascus, God told Ananias directly:

> Do you have a mission statement? How confident are you in it? What confirmation have you received for it? How long could you keep working with that mission if you, like Paul, traveled on and on with no new affirmations?

> "This man is my chosen instrument to carry my name before the Gentiles and their kings and before the people of Israel. I will show him how much he must suffer for my name" (Acts 9:15-16).

Paul knew that he and Silas had the gifts needed to carry out this mission. Once they started, there was no reason to consult their design again—Paul clearly had the gifts of teaching and apostleship. Paul also trusted that his passion for checking back to nurture the churches he had founded was God-given.

Paul learned from the circumstances at Antioch. There, the church had been greatly encouraged by the decision of the Council, so Paul took that as evidence to spread word of the decision to the other churches. Because it also helped Lystra and Derbe, Paul viewed the message's reception as an "open door" to continue.

> In your situation, what skills or gifts are key? Do your gifts match the needs or do you have doubts over whether God views you as qualified for the task?

Paul watched for the Holy Spirit. Paul had gone as far as Iconium on his first missionary journey and no doubt was anxious to continue on to new frontiers, the regions of Phrygia and Galatia. However, he paid attention to the Holy Spirit. The text doesn't say just what the Holy Spirit did to keep Paul from turning north or south, but he continued heading west.

God did not give them a master plan when they started out on this journey; Paul's purpose was to visit churches they had planted, but they weren't handed a set itinerary. And the itinerary they chose took them back to their enemies, not just old friends—Paul was stoned and left for dead on his previous visit to Lystra.

However, because he knew his particular calling was to plant new churches, Paul kept moving after he'd fulfilled his first purpose, alert for where his next platform might be. Paul walked around three hundred miles with no clear idea of where he was going. Just "No, not here. Not here, either." And his patience and perseverance were eventually rewarded with a clear vision. We know Paul's companions were relieved to get marching orders—note that they "got ready at once to leave for Macedonia"—but they were never paralyzed by uncertainty.

It's as if they kept moving by trusting the first three guidance systems—the biblical foundation of their mission, their own giftedness for the task, and the circumstances that led them toward new places to preach the Gospel. And in Macedonia, they could look back over their long journey knowing they'd taken the right path.

Finding God's Guidance in the Midst of Grief

> *What do you do when life hands you the worst you can imagine and you have to build a new future? When death or illness or betrayal or natural disaster bombard your life? At these times we are often vulnerable to faulty thinking and are simply not at our best. How can we safely move ahead? How do we listen for God in the darkest of times, be certain that what we're hearing is of God and not the product of our own desires, and seek counsel from others without turning from what we believe God has said to us?*

Michelle believed in a God who loved her and who wanted to be in relationship with her long before she married. And her marriage was founded on faith. Even after the children were born, Michelle often waited up for Pat to return from the restaurant they owned. Together they shared a candlelight dinner as they nurtured their relationship. When her husband was diagnosed with manic depression, she prayed frequently, learned to recognize what caused his mood swings, and supported him as best she could. They were deeply in love, emotionally, physically, and spiritually. But when one of the periods of depression got out of control, Pat took his own life.

After the funeral, as the numbness of grief wore off, Michelle had little time for her own needs; her three daughters, ages five, three, and two, needed her. But the bottom had dropped out of her life and she felt like she was free-falling toward nothingness. During one of those first empty nights alone as she sobbed uncontrollably, Michelle remembered a favorite verse:

> My help comes from the Lord, the Maker of heaven and earth. He will not let your foot slip—he who watches over you will not slumber. (Psalm 121:2-3)

Michelle felt in a new way that God, too, was awake as she cried. She wasn't alone. The nights were still the worst times for her, but she concentrated on remembering the other promises she could claim.

> A father to the fatherless, a defender of widows, is God in
> his holy dwelling. (Psalm 68:5)

> "Fear not, for I have redeemed you; I have summoned you
> by name; you are mine" (Isaiah 43:1).

> "With man this is impossible, but with God all things are
> possible" (Matthew 19:26).

> And my God will meet all your needs according to his
> glorious riches in Christ Jesus. (Philippians 4:19)

Michelle started keeping track of how God was meeting her needs: spiritual, physical, financial, and emotional. The memorial funds covered the funeral expenses. People from their church brought meals for weeks on end, a tremendous help since Pat had done most of their cooking. Others she'd never met reached out to her at just the right times. A support group formed to help widows and widowers understand how children grieve, an understanding she desperately needed.

As the answered needs mounted, she gained confidence to pray about the bigger future. Was she paying more attention to what people wanted her to do or what God might have in mind? Could she keep their house? Should she go back to work or rely on her parents for a few years? Instead of listening to the constraints of traditional thinking, she started talking earnestly to God about her future.

One night during prayer, God seemed to speak to her. "Consider yourself. What do you need to flourish?" Relief washed over Michelle as she gave herself permission to think about her own needs. *Me? I don't want to go it alone. I'm the kind who has to talk it out to know what I'm thinking. I enjoy things when I can share them with someone else. And I'm too young to say a permanent good-bye to the romance and intimacy Pat and I shared. I want my daughters to*

What do you need to flourish? What might society chide you for in times of grief?

*have a new father, hopefully before they begin to depend on me
so much that remarriage would make them feel as if they'd lost
their mom as well as their dad.*

Knowing that most people would think she should wait, probably for years, before remarrying, Michelle looked for biblical
principles and saw God's desire for intact families whenever
possible. God as heavenly Father could care for her girls, but
ideally they should have an earthly father as well.

Michelle simply wasn't a loner. Even during the week right after
Pat had died, she'd made herself get out and be with others. She
went to church, repeating to herself that God was with her as she
squirmed under the stares of people who knew her only as
"that poor widow." She accepted invitations from couples who
had been "their" friends. Within just a few months of Pat's death,
she knew God was telling her, "Be true to how I made you. You
are to be married again."

This wasn't just wishful thinking; God made it clear to her that
her future didn't include being a single mom—so clear that
she almost expected her new husband to simply drop into her
life complete with a halo and references straight from heaven.
However, she soon took a dose of reality and began to list the
difficulties she faced. She knew how great marriage could be;
this couldn't be second-best. Again, she turned to the promises
of God: "Cast all your anxiety on him because he cares for
you" (1 Peter 5:7).

"Okay, God," she said. "I'm glad you're there because our future
is safer in your hands than in mine. I'm going to tell you exactly
what I think I need. First, it isn't enough that I have a husband;
my girls need a father as well.

Second, we're still so vulnerable and fragile. I can't do anything
that might hurt them or me. And while after all of this I know
you'll take care of me, I still want someone I can lean on, so make
him tall—and why not dark and handsome, since I'm listing all
of this out. Please, too, give him a steadiness and a calm manner, in contrast to Pat's illness. And above all, he has to be a
Christian. There can't be many like that out there—and if there
are any, why would they want to be saddled with all of us? Help

me recognize what you have in mind for me."

As she worked through her own fears and emotions, she wondered what her friends would think if she started to date.

They thought she was crazy. She might have thought so too if she hadn't been so earnest in prayer, but feeling the disapproval of her friends was extremely difficult for Michelle, who usually acted as a peacemaker. A few, though, understood, as did the minister she met with for grief counseling. He cautioned her strongly but said, "I know you've asked for God's protection and guidance in this. Just keep up the prayer if your white knight really does seem to appear."

> On what issues might you struggle to follow God in spite of the disapproval of friends? The type of work you do? Where you live? The choices of how you use your leisure or volunteer time?

And she did. She asked the friends she trusted most to arrange a blind date for her *only* if they thought there was a chance for a serious relationship. The two or three she accepted were pleasant enough, but she felt that they were only interested in her. None mentioned anything about her situation or even asked about her daughters. While she certainly didn't want to dwell on her problems, their total lack of interest seemed a warning to her.

She was so convinced, though, that God wanted her to remarry that she even gathered up the courage to call the brother-in-law of a friend when she couldn't seem to rid herself of the idea.

> On which side might you err—dismissing these indicators as coincidence or taking them as a sign from God and not checking for further guidance?

A few people had mentioned that Tom was thoughtful and kind. Even as she dialed the phone she thought, *This is too much. What am I going to say? "Hey, I need a husband"?*

However, a few nights later when Tom came to her door, she couldn't help but tick off her prayer list. Tall, dark, handsome…. He introduced himself and then said, "It's so quiet—where are your girls?"

When Michelle explained that her parents had taken them for the evening, he seemed genuinely disappointed. "Could I see a picture of them?" As he looked at their Christmas photo, he asked a few questions about their ages and schooling. The contrast was startling—her other dates hadn't even asked their names. *God, she prayed silently, is this really someone who would be interested in all four of us, not just me?*

In those first dates, Tom seemed to know what to say and when to listen—and he was an incredible listener. He told Michelle, "I don't want to act as if Pat had never been a part of your life, so I have to understand the hole that's been left in you and the girls." He made it clear early on that he enjoyed being with all of them. "You don't always have to find a sitter. We can just as well talk while we play with the girls." So they did. Tom sat and colored with them, agreed to watch children's movies, even put bandages on their cuts. The girls looked forward to his visits.

Michelle knew quickly from all of her considerations of their vulnerabilities that she either had to commit herself to Tom or break things off before the girls formed too much of an attachment. But how would she know if Tom was really the one?

Certainly she was attracted to him, but that wasn't enough for marriage. And the girls liked him well enough, but that didn't mean he was ready to go from bachelorhood to fatherhood in one move.

> Have you analyzed where you are most vulnerable? What weakness might get you into the most trouble in your decision?

As she prayed and watched him, Michelle realized that the best guidance from God was who Tom was.

He showed up after the first ice storm of the season and cleared her steps and driveway. When the snow melted, he came over so early one morning that he managed to finish cleaning the yard up from the doings of her German shepherd before she knew he was there. He thought of places the girls might want to go and he volunteered to baby-sit. And when she told him one evening that her youngest had fallen off a swing and gone to the emergency room for stitches he said, "Why didn't you call me at work? I'd have gone with you or taken the other girls."

While Michelle *didn't* have a vision or hear a voice to confirm that marrying Tom was God's will for her, she had a list of criteria and needs she had made before ever meeting him. She knew that he was praying about whether he was ready to be her husband and father to three girls. Michelle also knew that love is action. And as she watched Tom act out his love for all four of them, she knew that she could trust her heart to him. They married a little over a year after the death of her first husband.

It doesn't take much to point out how Michelle relied on all four guidance systems. She already knew God's promises. She paid attention to God's direct leadings. Those led her to carefully consider her own design and readiness for remarriage. And she paid attention to circumstances: Tom's interest in her girls from the first moment he came to her door. Both of them looked to these affirmations that God was with them as they set their wedding date amid the concerns and warnings of many of their friends.

Don't be shocked; we know the rest of the story: five years of loving marriage. They faced problems, but they learned to pray together. Their daughters felt fear at first in trusting a new person in their lives. They still missed their "Papa" and occasionally whined that Tom wasn't as fun. But as he let them be themselves, they eventually came to look at him as "Daddy" and opened their hearts to him as an individual, not a replacement for Pat. And they love their two new little brothers!

Finding Guidance in the Midst of Career Anxiety

With so many societal pressures trying to dictate what we should be, seeking clear guidance for our careers can be another dilemma. How do you know if you are to grow where you're planted or move on to new horizons? What do you do if your job is terminated? Have you missed God's plan? In an environment where few companies offer security, how do you plan your long-term future? What is God calling you to do?

Paul Bertleson didn't confine his activities as youth pastor to the hours scheduled for youth programs at his church; he was involved in the lives of those who attended. If they needed a heart-to-heart talk, he'd pick them up from school. Whether on retreats or mission trips, he was their willing servant as well as their leader, helping to pitch tents, find lost sunglasses, or simply encourage them when they struggled.

And Paul was constantly looking for activities or methods that would help the teenagers entrusted to him grow spiritually. Since he believed it's harder for God to guide idle people, Paul was willing to try new mission trips or other events as well as core study programs.

As the program at his own church grew, Paul felt keenly that teens at big churches generally had access to more opportunities than those at small churches. He wondered what would happen if he offered to share his resources and connections or to network smaller churches together to help them attain the critical numbers for many of the things teenagers enjoyed: Christian concerts, lock-ins or all-night events, or mission opportunities.

Paul sent flyers to about one thousand churches in his state. While some were interested in the entertainment ideas, over

> Paul had two central passions: getting teens connected with Christ and mission work. Do you have any passions that can guide you for career direction?

one hundred churches expressed an interest in mission trips. That first summer, four hundred kids from thirty-five churches joined together for several outreaches.

At about this time, the missions pastor position at Paul's church opened up. As he considered the various duties the job would entail, Paul realized that he was already concentrating most of his efforts on missions. He decided that by moving out of direct youth ministry and into direct mission work, he could encourage a broader section of his church to take part in mission projects. He still helped coordinate teen activities related to his missions responsibilities.

> If your career situation is forcing you to let go of a passion, is there a way to pursue that passion as a hobby or through volunteer work? Or is it time to honor another passion?

In addition, Paul's efforts to network with smaller churches was taking on a life of its own. Paul partnered with others in founding YouthWorks!, whose mission was to network small churches for missions. Paul served on its board while others ran the day-to-day operations.

Paul's expertise in youth ministry and in missions had all come from his hands-on experiences, not formal training. As missions pastor, he gained more of the formal education and traditional networks he had lacked. However, Paul's time was filled with committee meetings and administrative tasks. Finding the time to go on mission trips became increasingly difficult. While Paul knew that developing these new skills would be good in the long run and that his church's outreach program had flourished under his direction, he still felt dissatisfied.

> Have you been responsible for tasks or been forced to operate in environments that really frustrated you? If so, did you need to learn anything from those situations? Have you since needed the skills you developed?

To reconnect with the people he wanted to serve, Paul

plunged into an urban rehabilitation project his church sponsored. Then the executive director of YouthWorks! resigned and more of Paul's time went to that outreach. Because his unofficial work was more fulfilling than his job, Paul was on the edge of overcommitment. Then his youngest son was diagnosed with leukemia, and Paul knew he simply had too many balls in the air. Something had to go, but what?

Paul took a good look at his choices. Going full-time with YouthWorks! would allow him to go back to operating in his more entrepreneurial style instead of working through committees. Also, the demand for YouthWorks! services far exceeded their estimates; hundreds of churches were interested. However, Paul's position at church was stable and gave him a solid, well-known platform for developing programs and networking with others.

Paul easily could have been swayed here by his special design to move to YouthWorks! Circumstances pointed both to staying on as pastor for security or joining with success at YouthWorks! Paul knew he needed more guidance and looked to Scripture. He told us,

> In career decisions, do you find it easy to look for God's guidance in all four ways or do you tend to ignore any of the guidance systems?

Part of my understanding of doing the will of God came from a Bill Hybels sermon about the Israelites crossing the Jordan River. The river was at flood stage, yet God told Joshua to have the priests—the leaders—carry the Ark of the Covenant into the middle of the river. In other words, "Have the leaders step out in faith if you want to see what God can do." And when they did, the waters of the river stopped flowing. The priests stood on dry ground in the middle of the riverbed while Israel crossed over. (See Joshua 3-4.) I felt that God was asking me to step forward as a leader of YouthWorks! If I did so, we would see what God could do.

Two years later, Paul has few doubts that he listened well for God:

While the fact that we're sending 10,000 kids this summer
on different missions certainly affirms that we're within God's
will, even perhaps more important to me is the unmistakable
knowledge that I'm using all of my life experiences in this job.
I feel so affirmed in what I am doing because I can look back
and see why God took me into different situations and experi-
ences.

Again, Paul knew that both of his choices—staying on staff
at a church or going to YouthWorks! would help him carry out
Jesus' instructions for us to make disciples of others. With this
assurance, Paul took the story of crossing the Jordan and applied
it to his own life. He paid close attention to his own gifts and
design—he's more of an entrepreneur than an administrator.
Instead of setting his own agenda, he listened closely to the needs
of other churches and based the services of YouthWorks! functions on what he heard—he paid attention to the circumstances,
discerning which outreaches drew response and bore fruit.

"In retrospect," Paul says, "I can't believe this sort of organization wasn't founded ten years ago, the need is so great. But
then again, we might have been a bit intimidated if we'd really
known how our idea would take off. I think we gain the power
to do God's will as we step forward in faith, even if we can't
survey the final destination."

Moving Ahead With Confidence

Do you see how being well versed in the first two guidance
systems helped the apostle Paul, Michelle, and our friend Paul
to step out in faith? And how once they began to move, God
could provide more individual guidance?

Our *hope* is that reading these pages has shown you how to
gain this same confidence. Finding God's guidance isn't hard if
you start from the right set of assumptions, invest time in understanding who God is, what the Scriptures say, and how you are
designed.

Our *fear* is that our teachings might paralyze you, making you
think you have to stop and chart out what each of the four sys-

tems is saying before you take a single step forward. And that attitude simply isn't what the Bible teaches or what people who've learned to walk confidently have experienced.

If you're experiencing paralysis in a decision, back up and ask yourself, Why? What is causing you to be indecisive? Perhaps it isn't yet time to make a decision, but perhaps it's time to reconsider what your stumbling block might be:

- Have you truly learned to trust God to the point that you know your own ideas are second-best if they conflict with God's ideas?
- Have you committed time to knowing yourself and the Bible's wisdom?
- Are you with people who encourage you to look for God—especially in ways or through means that you might tend to scoff at?

Yes, we're repeating ourselves, but our central message to you is: *God wants to guide you. Demonstrate your trust and your sincerity. And even if you misstep, God will be waiting to get you back on track.*

At first I thought I couldn't move until I knew where
to go, but what I really need to know is where you are.
With me, around me, ahead of me, behind me,
inside me, to guide me
over unknown terrain,
past unseen dangers,
around traps and temptations,
in loss and gain,
to the center of your will.

I trust you, Lord,
with my heart, soul, and mind.
You guide me in love
whenever I look for you,
listen for you, talk with you,
seek you without ceasing.

Amen.

Reflections for Your Own LifeDirections

1. Look through our main points in this chapter. Which one caught your attention the most? Why?
   - While one system may be enough for simple decisions, in major decisions, analyze *why* you are ignoring any of the four systems God uses to guide you before dismissing its importance to that particular situation.
   - To use all four systems
     (a) Get as familiar as you can with *Scripture* and your *Special Design*.
     (b) Be open to direct leadings of the *Holy Spirit*, but be ready to keep moving without them.
     (c) Evaluate your *Circumstances*.

(d) Trust the gifts you have and their roles in guiding you.

(e) Work through your blind spots and vulnerabilities.

(f) Pray.

2. Chart the decision you selected in chapter 1 using this process. How did you do in integrating all four systems? How might you look for God's guidance differently now?

3. Which of the four guidance systems are you most likely to discard? Why? When has it gotten you into trouble?

4. The four guidance systems are our path to freedom in Christ. As you make choices, we point out, one of two things will happen. Either you'll look back a while later and say, "Even though there have been some bumps, I know I walked with God" or you'll turn around and say, "I guess it's time to change direction again, but thanks, God, for sticking with me the whole time." It may be months or even years before you know whether you really made a wrong choice or simply took a detour to gain a new skill or understanding. So don't agonize over it. Just keep looking for God and you'll still be in the right race.

Does this make sense to you? Why or why not?

Chapter 7

Flying in Formation:
Finding Guidance in Community

How very good and pleasant it is
when kindred live together in unity!

—Psalm 133:1 NRSV

Have you ever wondered how an entire flock of geese can stay on course as they migrate over thousands of miles? After all, they take turns being lead bird, shifting positions within their distinctive V-formation. You don't see them crashing into each other or following a wayward comrade off course.

Through mathematical analysis, scientists have recently begun to understand how a flock stays organized. When one member starts heading astray, the birds closest to it will also swerve, but not as severely as the first. As the error passes to other birds, they go off course even less, until finally the birds farthest back aren't affected at all. And the flock still heads in the right direction. There's safety in numbers. One bird alone can't take the flock off track; further, the flock keeps each member from straying.

But we also see beauty and strength when we gaze up at a migrating flock. And we hear them encouraging one another, honking to bolster the spirit of each. What if when the world looked at Christians they saw the same vision of oneness?

Can We Ever Flock Together?

One of the frequent themes in Paul's letters is Christian unity, which might be defined as a state of oneness, harmony, or accord. We are to function as a community—unified individuals within the body of Christ. And that comm*unity* has to be established and united *before* conflicts over direction or purpose arise.

Think about this: The Christian church isn't a democracy. God is at the head, making all the decisions. We're supposed to work together as the unified body of Christ to follow God's instructions. If your church, or prayer group, or mission team, or any other group of believers faces a decision and someone says, "Let's vote. Majority rules," tell them they're wrong (unless you're trying to decide which pizza delivery to use). Instead of taking a headcount, our responsibility is to work as a group to discern the will of God and then follow those directions together. Paul pleads, "Let the peace of God be the decider of all things within your hearts, for it is to that peace you were called, so that you might be united in one body" (Colossians 3:15).[1]

Of course, the easiest way to build unity is to simply exclude everyone who disagrees with the majority, but then you're building a clique, not a community. God gifted people in different ways within the body of Christ, and we are to respect those differences. In his book *A Different Drum*, M. Scott Peck points out,

> A friend correctly defined community as a "group that has learned to transcend its individual differences." But this learning takes time, the time that can be bought only through commitment. "Transcend" does not mean "obliterate" or "demolish." It literally means "to climb over." The achievement of community can be compared to the reaching of a mountaintop.[2]

---

1 William Barclay, *The Letters to the Philippians, Colossians, and Thessalonians,* 2nd edition (Philadelphia: The Westminster Press, 1959).

2 M. Scott Peck, *A Different Drum: Community-Making and Peace* (New York: Touchstone, 1988), 62.

Paul didn't say this was going to be easy, but he tells us what we need to be united and why it is so important:

> May the God who gives endurance and encouragement give you a spirit of unity among yourselves as you follow Christ Jesus, so that with one heart and mouth you may glorify the God and Father of our Lord Jesus Christ. (Romans 15:5-6)

A church that seeks guidance in unity glorifies God. However, Paul lets us know that such unity may take *endurance*. To succeed in this, we probably need endurance in two ways. First, making a unified decision where everyone is convinced that the choice is God's will may not be a quick process. Everyone involved is best off training for the long haul, building endurance that will help them be patient and persistent in seeking consensus. This isn't a resigned, quiet form of patience, but the kind that keeps working with all hope intact toward the goal of glorifying God. Second, *endurance* also means being able to withstand adversity or stress—now isn't that an apt description of many a congregational meeting! But that's why Paul also mentions *encouragement:* we are to inspire one another with courage and hope as we endeavor to come to a unified decision.

Close your eyes for a moment and imagine what your church would be like if it really operated that way. Everyone embracing the Sunday school curriculum. Teens, parents, and leaders harmoniously selecting missions destinations and regular activities. Total agreement on the quality and size of the organ. Paul tells us exactly what it would be like:

> Therefore, as God's chosen people, holy and dearly loved, clothe yourselves with compassion, kindness, humility, gentleness and patience. Bear with each other and forgive whatever grievances you may have against one another. Forgive as the Lord forgave you. And over all these virtues put on love, which binds them all together in perfect unity. Let the peace of Christ rule in your hearts, since as members of one body you were called to peace. (Colossians 3:12-15)

The world would flood our doors if we actually operated as Paul pleads. And the path to this kind of unity? The same four guidance systems we've shown you are key to corporate guidance. With compassion, kindness, humility, gentleness, and patience, we can together search the Scriptures to establish the principles God desires that we apply together. In love, we can look at the unique gifts and passions of our members. With Christ in our hearts, we can listen for the direct leadings different people might receive and together evaluate what God might be saying in the circumstances surrounding the decisions we face.

Okay, we know it isn't that easy. After all, our own church just went through the process of deciding to build a new sanctuary. And we didn't always succeed in reaching unity. In fact, the struggle landed frequently on the front page of the local newspaper. But as the walls go up, we are still speaking to each other. Our human pride and fallibilities may have caused some disharmony along the way, but somehow we endured the process and are now encouraged by how things are moving along.

We really wouldn't suggest that you look to our church as an example of unity (although we can clue you in on what did and didn't work very well), but if you look at the church in the book of Acts, you can see how central all four guidance systems were to their unity and growth.

Guidance in the Early Church

The leaders of the early church seemed to know instinctively where to look for guidance from God.

The Bible. Right after Jesus' ascension, the disciples chose a replacement for Judas to conform with what they read in Psalm 109:8: "May another take his place of leadership." Their early preaching conveyed how Jesus had fulfilled what the prophets had written.

Their gifts and unique design. When the administrative tasks of running the early church became too much for the Twelve, they chose seven men based on their gifts of wisdom (Acts 6).

Direct leadings. The apostles saw them all, from angels orchestrating jailbreaks to visions on the roof, from dreams to direct commands. But if these clear signals were absent, they still kept moving.

Circumstances. When Paul first came to Jerusalem, the apostles were understandably concerned about the genuineness of his message, but once Barnabas convinced them of it, they welcomed him. And when circumstances held no good for Paul—the local Grecian Jews were plotting to kill him—they heeded those circumstances and sent him off to Tarsus (Acts 9). They didn't wait around to see if God would miraculously protect him.

However, corporately the early church also managed to integrate the use of the guidance systems, modeled perhaps most insightfully for us at the Council at Jerusalem. At issue was whether to circumcise Gentile converts to Christianity. The fact that the church never debates this issue anymore tells how successfully the early church resolved its dispute, but at the time, the conflict was as major as if your congregation were debating whether to do away with the celebration of Christmas or Communion.

Even though the dispute originated in Antioch, Paul and Barnabas were sent to Jerusalem so that the church could reach a unified decision on the subject. The fifteenth chapter of Acts tells us that the apostles and elders of the Jerusalem church discussed the issue at great length.

Then Peter, whose first outreach to the Gentiles followed the vision God had given him that nothing was unclean, got up and reminded them of how God had chosen him to speak to the Gentiles—a direct leading.

Paul and Barnabas then described their ministry to the Gentiles

and the miracles they had seen—the evidence was in the circumstances that showed God at work.

James then quoted from the Scriptures: "...that the remnant
of men may seek the Lord, and all the Gentiles who bear my
name" (Amos 9:11, as quoted by James in Acts 15:17) —biblical
wisdom.

While they may not have used considerations of their design
to make the decision, they chose messengers with the gift of
prophecy to deliver their decision to Antioch—Judas and Silas,
who were able to encourage and strengthen those who received
the message. In addition, the apostles—Paul, Peter, and James—
used their teaching and prophetic gifts to share their insights.

The apostles exhibited endurance and encouragement as
they worked through this issue—no snap decisions, no rush to
reach a conclusion before dinner. But more important, they
did everything within an atmosphere of prayer and worship:
"They devoted themselves to the apostles' teaching and to the
fellowship, to the breaking of bread and to prayer" (Acts 2:42).
The atmosphere was set for "bearing with one another in love.
Make every effort to keep the unity of the Spirit through the
bond of peace" (Ephesians 4:2-3).

It can be done. John Calvin, for all his work on doctrine,
declared,

> There ought to prevail among [Christians] such a reverence
> for the ministry of the word and the sacraments that wher-
> ever they perceive these things to be, there they must consider
> the church to exist...nor need it be of any hindrance that some
> points of doctrine are not quite so pure, seeing that there is
> scarcely any church which has not retained some remnants of
> former ignorance."[3]

The church can make a decision and walk out smiling, hand
in hand. But we have to walk in with compassion, kindness,
humility, gentleness, and patience. And love. And the peace of

3 John Calvin to William Farrell, from Strasbourg, 24 October 1538, in H. Beveridge and J.
Bonnet, eds., *Selected Books of John Calvin: Tracts and Letters*, vol. 4, trans. D. Constable
(Grand Rapids, Mich.: Baker Book House, 1983), 101-2.

Christ. And some churches have really done it.

In Cincinnati, Ohio, Steve Sjogren of the Vineyard Church had struggled for two years to plant a new church. The result? Thirty-seven members. As he prayed over what he was doing wrong, he heard God telling him, "You're boring and not worth joining. Get out there." He and his small flock decided that instead of inviting others to come in, they would go out. Serving rather than inviting met their values, these new ideas for outreach better fit their gifts, and all of them worked together to brainstorm acts of kindness they could engage in for others. Some of them raked leaves, others fed parking meters or wrapped presents at a mall at Christmastime, while still others scraped windshields or cleaned public rest rooms—all for free, no strings attached. And the church has grown almost too quickly for them to handle.

The original members acted in unity: they trusted Steve's message from God, they felt the decision was in harmony with how they were gifted, they found biblical support for their outreaches to the kinds of people Jesus sought, and they took into account the circumstances of the people they were trying to reach and what worked most effectively. Their united values include "Show, don't tell about God's love" and "Where the Spirit of the Lord is, there is fun." They've had to start at least ten more churches!

So how can you apply these principles in your family or work team or church or volunteer team?

Establishing the Ground Rules

The only way to build this framework is carefully. And the first step in that care is making sure that you agree on the ground rules far in advance of any decision-making process:

- Worship together.
- Study together.
- Pray together.
- Stay together.

Worship will focus attention on who is really in charge: God, not some appointed or self-appointed leader.

Study will gain consensus on how to navigate the Bible to discern the differences between principles, commandments, and areas that are disputable.

Prayer in unison helps clarify your purposes and listen for God's purposes. In silence, prayer also allows each individual to examine his or her motives or opinions and relinquish them if necessary.

Finally, by covenanting to stay together until you reach unity, you set the proper stage for enduring what may be a difficult search for God's will. It's much easier to walk out than to continue meeting until everyone feels a peace about the decision that can only come from God. As you covenant together, though, rejoice in the promise that Jesus is present whenever even two or three come together in his name. (See Matthew 18:20.)

Step One—Searching the Scriptures

The only difference between individual guidance from the Bible and corporate guidance is that there must be agreement within the community on how the Scriptures apply to the decision being made (remember, we said to start with worship and prayer). Following a set, objective procedure can help groups work through differences in interpretation.

1. Come to an agreement, based on Scripture, on what is disputable and nondisputable in the matter being discussed.

2. Look for biblical principles to support each of the alternatives the group could choose.

For this to work, opinions have to be buried in deference to Bible verses. Leadership authority or need to control has to take a backseat to objective analysis of different interpretations. Each point of view must be voiced without interruption or criticism. You could practice phrases such as "I hadn't thought of it that way before," "You may have a point there," or "That's an interesting interpretation."

There isn't much point in moving on unless you are in agreement on the foundation from which you will make the decision. "I appeal to you, brothers, in the name of our Lord Jesus Christ, that all of you agree with one another so that there may be no divisions among you and that you may be perfectly united in mind and thought" (1 Corinthians 1:10).

Step Two—Discern the Gifts, Values, and Passions of the Group

Given that most individuals don't know how they are gifted, it isn't surprising that most congregations don't know anything about the giftedness of their membership. Fortunately, as more and more laypeople are called to take part in the leadership of churches, congregations are seeing more examples of what happens when people act on their gifts and passions.

Sometimes in large congregations or groups, the gifts are so diverse that knowing them doesn't matter as much; the church could go in many directions. But what about a smaller congregation? After all, birds of a feather often flock together. If you've got a sanctuary full of people gifted with mechanical aptitude, you might want to think twice about where outreach efforts are directed. You don't want to be caught like one women's leader Jane knows who was telling the group what a deal she'd gotten on new curtains for their gathering place when one of those in attendance said, "But I'm a seamstress. I would have done it for free!"

Equally key are the passions of a group. The list of worthy possibilities for using resources, both financial and human, for the body of Christ is endless. And you can manipulate those passions in people—it's pretty hard not to reach for your checkbook when you see pictures of starving children or hear stirring testimonies of effective ministries. However, when a group already has worthy passions, is it God's will that those be superseded by others?

Jane used to belong to a church that concentrated on foreign missions. Children in that congregation grew up surrounded by missionaries home on furlough and stories of the differences they made in the quality of life for people in third world countries. Many members constantly looked for short-term missions opportunities, a phenomenal percentage of the congregation had actually served overseas, and even more gave generously to support the long list of missionaries the church sponsored. The congregation was united in its passion for providing tangible help to people overseas while spreading the Good News of Jesus.

Then the senior pastor decided that this passion was wrong. They should concentrate their resources on work in the troubled neighborhoods of their own city. Perhaps God was calling that minister to the inner city, but when he tried to persuade his flock that their overseas emphasis was misplaced, unity was lost.

This was an extreme case. There was no discussion of a biblical foundation for either emphasis. There certainly was no evaluation of the gifts and passions of the congregation. But even worse, no process was in place for the laying aside of egos and opinions to work together to discern God's will. It quickly became an all-out pastor vs. congregation dispute, and in this case, the pastor lost.

Can you imagine if this whole situation had been handled as modeled in the Council of Jerusalem? First, both sides might have presented, without interruption or criticism from the other, why they believed the church should choose a certain path.

Then, both sides could present the biblical evidence—and certainly the teachings of Jesus uphold both local and foreign missions.

Next, the group would prayerfully consider the circumstances surrounding the choices. Exactly how effective were the church's mission outposts? Were lives being changed? This would echo the concrete evidence Paul and Barnabas presented in Acts 15 to convince the council that God was converting the Gentiles and gifting them with the Holy Spirit even though they weren't circumcised.

Conversely, the pastor could present the circumstances that had persuaded him that the church needed to alter its course.

Both sides would then need to allow the other side to present alternative interpretations of those circumstances—remember, we are not the authors of our lives and may be blind to what is really going on.

Most importantly, at every stage of the process, both sides needed to work toward unity, asking for God's input if the group seemed off course. The evidence of true unity? The fruit of the Spirit. James tells us, "But the wisdom that comes from heaven is first of all pure; then peace-loving, considerate, submissive, full of mercy and good fruit, impartial and sincere" (James 3:17). If the "wisdom" the group is sharing isn't producing this sort of atmosphere, then God's wisdom isn't yet in evidence.

Does this sound too Utopian? Even impossible? Chuck Colson wondered about the wisdom of requiring total unity, too, when he first brought the idea of Prison Fellowship to England. A senior member of the British Parliament had invited Chuck and other leaders to present their ideas to a gathering of over three hundred chaplains, ministers, and laypeople already involved in prison ministries. After a day and a half of presentations and discussion, Chuck was relieved when the vote to begin Prison Fellowship England was almost unanimous. Only a dozen people opposed the proposal. Chuck turned to go home, his mission over, but the leader banged the gavel and said that action would be delayed until they could meet again, saying, "If this be of the Holy Spirit...He will say the same thing to all of us. And if it is not God's doing, we want no part of it."[4]

Six months later the same three hundred reassembled, the vote was unanimous, and Prison Fellowship England is one of the strongest of the ministries Chuck has founded. Reflecting back, Chuck said,

> Disunity in the church would be understandable if Christianity were simply a relationship. Jesus and me. In that case, of course, everyone's experience would be different. Disunity would be understandable if Christianity were nothing more than a set of creeds and confessions. But

---

4 Charles Colson, *The Body* (Nashville: Word Publishing, 1992), 108. All rights reserved.

Christianity is more than these. It is centered in the One who professes to be ultimate reality, the personal God who gives us life and meaning and who calls us to be His body at work in the world. If we really understand this, disunity becomes impossible.[5]

So What Can Go Wrong?

As in individual guidance, we are not perfect, nor do we live in a perfect world. Leaders can manipulate. Followers can refuse to rethink their positions. Most of us are much better at trying to do our will in God's name than at "being like-minded, having the same love, being one in spirit and purpose. Do nothing out of selfish ambition or vain conceit, but in humility consider others better than yourselves. Each of you should look not only to your own interests, but also to the interests of others" (Philippians 2:2-4).

We are human. We will sometimes fail to see together what God has in mind. And even in the early church, when the teachings of Jesus were so fresh in everyone's mind and the people of The Way were drawn together through persecution, unity sometimes eluded them. Even Paul and Barnabas fought, finally parting ways over whether John Mark, who had pulled out in the middle of a missionary journey, could rejoin their efforts.

You see, unity isn't about appeasement, but about love. And while corporate guidance through unity is the ideal, our human failings may sometimes block its coming to fruition. An emergency, a deadline, or stubborn inflexibility may make unity impossible. There are times when you *cannot* convince the other side that they neglected to listen for God and you *cannot* always say, "Well, I'll let it go this time. Better to have peace than to have you unhappy." However, before you go your own way, pray again about who is really wrong.

Admitting we were wrong or wishy-washy, as Peter did when Paul found him hesitating to eat with the Gentiles, brings us one

---

5 Ibid., 108-9.

step closer to the ideal of unity. Paul encourages us, for the glory of God to

> Do everything without complaining or arguing, so that you may become blameless and pure, children of God without fault in a crooked and depraved generation, in which you shine like stars in the universe as you hold out the word of life. (Philippians 2:14-16)

What would the world think of us if we truly operated that way?

Being listeners
Being of one heart and mind
Seeking you
Seeking unity
Finding your will
Finding peace
We ask this in your name
We ask this to glorify you
Amen.

Reflections for Your Own LifeDirections

1. Look through our main points for this chapter. Which one catches your attention the most? Why?
   • The Christian church is headed by God. Decisions are to be made in unity, not in a democratic manner.
   • Unity takes endurance and mutual encouragement.
   • To achieve unity, the church needs to worship, study, pray, and stay together.
   • Groups are to use the same four systems in seeking God's guidance.
   • Unity isn't appeasement but finding God's will.

2. Which of these is hardest for you in working toward unity? How might you improve?
   - Taking time for corporate worship
   - Remaining open to other interpretations as you study
   - Praying, either aloud or silently, to rethink your own or the group's decisions
   - Enduring, having the patience to work toward unity

3. James tells us, "But the wisdom that comes from heaven is first of all pure; then peace-loving, considerate, submissive, full of mercy and good fruit, impartial and sincere" (James 3:17). How might you grow in that kind of wisdom?

4. Are you more vulnerable to seeking appeasement or to not
   rethinking your own position? Meditate on 1 Corinthians 1:10
   for guidance in how you might be more helpful in seeking
   corporate guidance:

   > I appeal to you, brothers, in the name of our Lord Jesus
   > Christ, that all of you agree with one another so that there
   > may be no divisions among you and that you may be perfectly
   > united in mind and thought. (1 Corinthians 1:10)

Chapter 8

All in God's Good Timing:
A Few Final Guiding Thoughts

Commit your way to the Lord; trust in him and he will do this:
He will make your righteousness shine like the dawn,
the justice of your cause like the noonday sun.

—Psalm 37:5-6

Perhaps you still envy those flocks of birds navigating toward warmer climates. Their instincts guide them without fail to the right destination. They never seem to choose the wrong flyway. Birds just know what they're supposed to do; they don't have thoughts and feelings and doubts that can blind them to the way they are to go. But consider this: Birds don't have the freedom to choose their destination. Year after year they go from A to B and back to A again. If they've always gone to Capistrano, they don't have the option of investigating Florida or Mexico.

While using the guidance systems God has given us requires preparation, patience, and persistence, we have the freedom to direct our course as well as God's trust that we are able to do so. Finding God's guidance is an ongoing walk that takes place on our journey through this life. As we close, we hope to help you move from believing God guides us in these ways to working comfortably with these systems. Remember, God wants to guide us, but we need to place ourselves where we can discern those leadings. Peter Marshall prayed,

Give us the faith to believe that when God wants us to do or not to do any particular thing, God finds a way of letting us know it. May we not make it more difficult for Thee to guide us, but be willing to be led of Thee, that Thy will may be done in us and through us.[1]

Getting to where God can guide us easily takes preparation. You have to invest time to know God and know yourself so you can be led through the first two guidance systems. There's no way around this. And we also know that finding time in this age of busy schedules sounds impossible. However, the alternative is wasting time backing up from the mistakes you'll inevitably make if you aren't prepared to discern how God is guiding you.

In any planning process, the preparatory work is at least as important as the final decisions you make. When Jane helps a company prepare a strategic plan, she spends more time listening to the owners and managers to discern their aspirations and concerns than she does helping them set goals. If that groundwork isn't properly laid, they'll come up with a plan, but it won't be one they have ownership in. If you want God's hand in your planning, listen first.

Persistence. Remember, finding God's will isn't a one-time event but something we do constantly for the little and big things in our lives. While none of us wants to be paralyzed by constant analysis of whether we're in or out of God's will, we can question, "Did I remember to ask for God's guidance in this matter before I raced on ahead?"

Perhaps *diligence* describes best the kind of effort and attitude you need; *Webster's* defines the diligent as those who are "characterized by steady, earnest, and energetic application and effort."

"I love those who love me, and those who seek me find me" (Proverbs 8:17).

---

[1] Peter Marshall, *Mr. Jones, Meet the Master* (Old Tappan, N.J.: Fleming H. Revell Company, 1950), 33.

Patience. People who truly listen for God act with one eye on the present and another on eternity, understanding God's guidance within the framework of the fullness of time. They can wait for this moment's answer because they already know the end of the story.

> Everyone who competes in the games goes into strict train-ing. They do it to get a crown that will not last; but we do it to get a crown that will last forever. Therefore I do not run like a man running aimlessly. (1 Corinthians 9:25-26)

Train yourself by practicing now to look for God, before you need guidance for a major decision.

Are you working with God in this or making it more diffi-cult for God to guide you? It's tough to put aside those pre-conceived notions of either how your life should go or how God should speak to you, but that's what it means to trust your Creator. Oswald Chambers pointed out that if we yield ourselves, turn ourselves over, God knows what we are to be:

> Let Him put you on His wheel and whirl you as He likes, and as sure as God is God and you are you, you will turn out exactly in accordance with the vision. Don't lose heart in the process.[2]

If you want to work *with God,* to yield yourself to that vision of all you can be, here's how you might approach today, tomor-row, next week, and the months, seasons, and years ahead.

For Each and Every Today

In the many examples we've given from people of the Bible to ordinary men and women of today, one of the common threads of those who walk easily with God is their steady diet of prayer and Scripture reading. Because they regularly placed themselves before God, they were ready to receive guidance.

We know that many of you question the feasibility of read-

---

[2] Oswald Chambers, *My Utmost for His Highest* (Oswald Chambers Publications Association, 1963), July 6 entry.

ing the Bible daily—either your hours are already so full that it's hard to read through your mail, or you've tried before without success. Perhaps you can't make yourself feel spiritual simply because your daily planner says that fifteen minutes are set aside for the purpose of a quiet time.

If this describes your thoughts, set an attainable goal. Included in the way God designed you were ways that you learn best, worship best, pray best, and study best. Find a method for delving into the Bible that lets you be diligent—"steady, earnest and energetic." If this sounds all but impossible, do three things for yourself:

1. Research a variety of spiritual practices that might suit you. Jane's book *SoulTypes: Finding the Spiritual Path That Is Right for You* highlights the most natural spiritual practices for each psychological type and what can actually push each type away from God.

   For each of us—even though we are all trying to understand the same truths—certain methods are more effective than others for seeking God. Some of you might join a group, some will study alone. You might learn through debate, while others would rather attend a lecture. With today's resources, your options are almost limitless: memorize songs, listen to the Bible on tape, use a daily devotional, post verses in your kitchen—to mention just some of them. If this is new for you, what is important is not how much you commit to, but that you commit to something that you will do.

2. Define *regular* for yourself. Instead of setting a standard that is doomed to failure, start with small steps so you can experience the guidance that comes from the Bible. A daily time may work if your days fit a pattern, but fewer and fewer people are regulated by the set schedules that once prevailed on factories and farms. Maybe your Mondays are wide open, but Tuesday starts with an early meeting and continues until you finish wiping down tables at a local soup kitchen. Find some *regular* times within the structure of your weeks.

3. Partner with someone for accountability. You might seek
out a spiritual director—someone who will help you to grow
spiritually—or covenant with a friend to set goals together and
hold each other accountable.

While God can certainly speak through magazines and books
other than the Bible, some of this regular time must go to the
Bible if you are to use the first guidance system.

For Each and Every Tomorrow

Just like reading the Bible, using the second guidance system
of knowing yourself takes preparation. *LifeKeys* (or however you
grasp how God has designed you) isn't a one-time thing but
an ongoing process if you want God to be able to guide you
through how you were created.

When we teach a *LifeKeys* class, we ask people to write that day's
date on the sheet where they summarize their gifts, values, and
passions. That way, they can look back, think about what has
changed since they wrote out their *LifeKeys,* and what might need
reconsideration. Remember, while your gifts, talents, and personality are constant, God can guide you through your changing
values and passions. As you come to crossroads in your life—as
well as for fresh insights periodically—reconsider your values.
Reconsider your passions. Is God trying to tell you anything?

But *LifeKeys* serves another purpose for guidance: It helps you
perform all the groundwork for writing a mission statement.

> It's in Christ that we find out who we are and what we are
> living for. Long before we first heard of Christ and got our
> hopes up, he had his eye on us, had designs on us for glori-
> ous living, part of the overall purpose he is working out in
> everything and everyone. (Ephesians 1:11-12 THE MESSAGE)

You can't determine your mission—what you are living for—
apart from Jesus. Not only are we a part of his overall purposes, but being part of it all is the ticket to glorious living.
Discovering all of this is worth any amount of preparation.

For most people, it takes weeks or even months to formulate a mission. They need the foundation of not just knowing their *LifeKeys,* but liking and appreciating what they have been given. It takes time to consider all the different roles you play and what kind of mission might connect or balance these roles.

> *I knew that David had drafted and redrafted his mission state-ment over a period of nine months before finally being inspired with the final wording during an afternoon alone in a hotel room, out of town.*
>
> *I'd been teaching the classes that became LifeKeys for three years and hadn't come up with one. Then one day as I listened to David teach this topic, as I'd heard him do many times before, I began to think back through how I'd chosen various writing and volunteer projects—and I knew what my mission was:* To help others reach their full potential, giving them tools and models to successfully continue the process on their own.
>
> *Those are the kinds of books I write—tools, not cut-and-dried answers. That's what I try to do as a mom—not do everything for my kids, but teach them principles or a process. It's what I do as a consultant—I don't want the managers depending on me to solve their problems, instead I want to give them communi-cation tools and techniques for working through their differences.*
>
> *When I'm asked to do something—for work or elsewhere, I ask whether it fits with my mission, with what I can do best for God. If not, I have good reason to say no unless it's one of those desperate needs that requires many people.*
>
> —Jane

Consider your mission statement your effort to act on the proverb "The human mind plans the way, but the Lord directs the steps" (Proverbs 16:9 NRSV). Jesus can give you a vision of all you were meant to be—just as he did for Peter, for the woman at the well, and for countless others in the Bible and through-out time.

Finding Balance in the Weeks Ahead

God wants us to have time for everything—everything, that is, for which we are responsible. We weren't given boundless energy. In fact, even God needed a day of rest, and we are commanded to rest as well. We can arrange our lives to accomplish that sort of balance or we can become trapped in a downward spiral, as Isaiah warned the Israelites:

> Very well then, with foreign lips and strange tongues God will speak to this people, to whom he said, "This is the resting place, let the weary rest"; and, "This is the place of repose"—but they would not listen. So then, the word of the Lord to them will become:

> Do and do, do and do,
> rule on rule, rule on rule;
> a little here, a little there—
> so that they will go and fall backward,
> be injured and snared and captured. (Isaiah 28:11-13)

Not taking time to rest—failing to care for your own limited resources of physical, emotional, and spiritual energy—results in a never-ending whirlwind of draining duty. Your mission statement, prayerfully conceptualized, provides focus and helps you discern those things you are living for. If you don't define it for yourself, other people will be all too glad to do it for you! Remember the story of Mary and Martha?

> As Jesus and his disciples were on their way, he came to a village where a woman named Martha opened her home to him. She had a sister called Mary, who sat at the Lord's feet listening to what he said. But Martha was distracted by all the preparations that had to be made. She came to him and asked, "Lord, don't you care that my sister has left me to do the work by myself? Tell her to help me!"

> "Martha, Martha," the Lord answered, "you are worried and upset about many things, but only one thing is needed. Mary has chosen what is better, and it will not be taken away from her" (Luke 10:38-42).

Martha wanted to set Mary's agenda for her, didn't she? Martha was only looking at *chronos*—chronological time. That meant, "Mary if you don't help me right now, dinner won't be ready in time. You can listen to Jesus later—and better yet, if you set the table, I'll be able to hear what he has to say, too."

Mary was looking at *kairos*—the fullness of time. That meant, "I have an opportunity to hear God right now, a chance that seldom comes. With a view to eternity, the most important thing I can do now is listen." Mary's *chronos* choices were based on her understanding of *kairos*. That's what a mission statement can do for you.

Once you have that mission statement, the second two guidance systems can break the hold that *chronos* has on you and point out what is most needed at the moment. Each and every day, there are things that simply must be done, such as eating and sleeping and taking care of those people and things for which you are responsible. But everyone around you will keep adding to your list if you don't make it yourself. Guarding that list and what it contains isn't selfish, but the only method we know that ensures that you respond only to those urgent requests that are actually important so you have time to fulfill your mission—which is eternally important but can play second fiddle to the demands of everyday living.

Your circumstances create the urgent, but the other guidance systems can help you filter the urgent to allow for the important.

Balancing the Seasons

What is important changes for each of us. These guidance systems help you discern these changes best when you are able to recognize the changing seasons of your life. We are told, "There is a time for everything, and a season for every activity under heaven" (Ecclesiastes 3:1). As you look for God's guidance, ask yourself what kind of season you're in.

Some seasons define God's will for you.

Some seasons are a waiting place, not a final destination.

Understanding the seasons of life helps you know what you can and cannot change.

Seasons of illness, seasons of parenting, seasons of learning—these can sometimes be all of the guidance you need, calling for you to concentrate your efforts on the tasks these seasons require.

> As a young mother, I had to redefine my mission. I wanted to continue the volunteer positions I had held and the significant contributions I made to my professional association. I thought if I simply tried harder, I could rearrange my schedule to do it all. Instead, I ended up feeling guilty and frustrated.
>
> Finally I realized that my mission of opening the hearts of others, letting them see those around them through the eyes of Jesus, could apply to my own children right now. It was okay with God if I concentrated on these four little people under my care during these years. My "mass" mission could go on hold for a while.
>
> —Teresa, 36, homemaker

Thus, just by understanding the season of your life, you can gain guidance from God.

As usual, with that said, we need to add a caution: Sometimes we're too likely to use the season of our life as an excuse. Our view of responsibility can get in the way of God's guidance. While we believe that taking your responsibilities seriously is part of how God guides you through circumstances, we also know that Jesus didn't always ask people to do what seemed the responsible thing. Peter, John, James, and Andrew left their fishing boats, their only sources of income. Matthew gave up collecting taxes. Again, a prayerful consideration of all four guidance systems, with counsel from those who have your best interest in mind, can help you discern what God is telling you.

All of us spend time in seasons of waiting, where we just aren't sure what God would have us do. Perhaps you struggle to reconcile your current circumstances with what you believe is God's plan for your life.

When you enter such a season (and it happens to all of us), take a good look at what you can and cannot change.

- Are you open to what God might have to say to you? Like Joseph, who learned while he waited?
- Are you being kind to yourself? Allowing yourself to recover from hurts or allowing yourself to prepare for what God has in mind next?
- Are you listening, holding lightly to your own dreams because God's plans are perfect?

If not, are you berating yourself for losing your way, failing to find God's plan for your life? Please remember what God repeats over and over:

> No matter how or why you stumble,
> God stands ready to show you how to
> return to what you were created to be.

No sin or wrongdoing can keep you from God's plans for you—just as the potter can reshape a marred pot, so God can reshape your life. (See Jeremiah 18:4-6.)

If the sins of others crush your dreams, God can bring new life: "You intended to harm me, but God intended it for good to accomplish what is now being done, the saving of many lives" (Genesis 50:20).

If the stress and anxiety of a situation is with you, God is with you: "When you pass through the waters, I will be with you; and when you pass through the rivers, they will not sweep over you. When you walk through the fire, you will not be burned; the flames will not set you ablaze" (Isaiah 43:2).

If it seems that Satan is doing his best to corrupt you, God is still guarding you: "Satan has asked to sift you as wheat. But I have prayed for you...that your faith may not fail" (Luke 22:31-32).

If the pain of the present seems too great to bear, look to the future with God: " 'For I know the plans I have for you,' declares the Lord, 'plans to prosper you and not to harm you, plans to give you hope and a future'" (Jeremiah 29:11).

God pleads with you to remember that you can always return

and look afresh for guidance. Wherever you are standing—close to God or far away, in trust or in doubt, in confusion or with confidence—someone else has been there before you, asking the same questions of God and wondering where to turn. The Bible, the church around you, the stories of the heroes of our faith, are packed with people who struggled to find God's will. But as they placed their trust in God, practiced what they knew to be true, and learned from those who had gone before them, they found that they could hear God. And discover God's perfect plans for their lives.

> Therefore, since we are surrounded by such a great cloud of witnesses, let us throw off everything that hinders and the sin that so easily entangles, and let us run with persever-ance the race marked out for us. (Hebrews 12:1)

You don't have to do it alone.
God is with you.
Others have gone before you and found the way.
Those who have already run the race
are cheering you on.
God's best to you.
May you soar with confidence
this side of heaven.

Reflections for Your Own LifeDirections

1. Look back through our main points for this chapter. Which one catches your attention the most? Why?
   - Using God's four guidance systems takes preparation, persistence, and patience.
   - For God to speak to you through these systems, you have to make space for God today and as you plan for the future.
   - Knowing your mission, if you form it while listening for God, can give you a constant vision of what being guided by God looks like for you.
   - The urgent needs of each day—the *chronos* moments—will crowd out listening for God—the *kairos* moments—unless you are focused.
   - All of us have seasons, or roles we are called to play, that may either change or dictate our mission.

2. Are the demands of your *chronos* days getting in the way of your *kairos* moments? What needs to take a backseat if you are going to make more room to listen for God?

3. In this chapter, Teresa talks about how her role as a mother changed the focus of her mission. What roles are you currently called to play? How might God be guiding you through those roles? What are you being asked to do? How does that differ from your longer-term passions? Are there ways to avoid frustration by changing your focus?

4. We talked about different seasons in life. What season are you in? Is it a season of frustration or waiting? How might it fit into God's full plan for your life?

Discover the Keys to Life...

LifeKeys is a revolutionary new approach to self-discovery—determining all you were created to be so you can live effectively for God. Most personality "tests" or spiritual gift inventories look at only one or two elements of who you are. *LifeKeys* looks at five elements, including your personality, values, talents, passions, and spiritual gifts. Ideal for group or individual use.

LifeKeys
—Jane A.G. Kise, David Stark, Sandra Krebs Hirsh *$14.99*

- Helps you choose a career, ministry, talent, and pastimes that offer satisfaction and maximize your potential.

- **Workbook** (*$6.99*) offers the excercises of *LifeKeys* in an easy-to-use, economical format.

> **"LifeKeys *makes it practically impossible not to come away with a profound sense that God created you uniquely, values you highly, and has good works in mind for you. I recommend* LifeKeys *for anyone seeking to integrate faith and life."***
> —Janet O. Hagberg, Author of *The Critical Journey*

Find Your Fit: LifeKeys for Teens
—Jane A.G. Kise and Kevin Johnson *$10.99*

- Provides youth leaders, counselors, parents, and Christian schools with a resource to help guide their teens through tumultuous times.

- Features exercises, quizzes, spiritual gifts inventories and more created specifically for older teens grappling with difficult questions of identity and God's place for them in the world.

- **Workbook** (*$6.99*) Presents the talent, interest, and personality discovery exercises of the *Find Your Fit* in an engaging manner.

> **"We wish we'd had this book when we were 17!"**
> —Sigmund Brouwer & Cindy Morgan, bestselling author and Dove Award-winning recording artist

BETHANY HOUSE PUBLISHERS
11400 Hampshire Ave. South
Minneapolis, MN 55438
www.bethanyhouse.com

Available from your local bookstore or from Bethany House Publishers.

For information on how you can teach LifeKeys in your church or organization, visit www.lifekeys.com or call (612)935-7591.

Appendix A

A Checklist of Life Gifts and Spiritual Gifts

B elow are lists of the life gifts and spiritual gifts, with definitions, as used in *LifeKeys*. You might use these lists to grasp the wide variety of talents and gifts God gives or to review ones you've previously identified.

However, if you've never completed a self-discovery process such as *LifeKeys*, we urge you to go much deeper than these simple lists allow.

Check below (✓) if one or more of these is your gift.

Realistic Life Gifts[1]

- ☐ Mechanical aptitude—able to understand and apply the principles of mechanics/physics
- ☐ Operating heavy equipment, driving—construction equipment as well as transportation vehicles

---

1 *LifeKeys* groups life gifts within the six interest areas delineated in John Holland's theory of the world of work. This theory was used to construct the Strong Interest Inventory™ as well as in major job classification systems.

- ☐ Manual dexterity—skill and ease at using one's hands or fine tools
- ☐ Building mechanical/structural devices—able to design and/or assemble materials as well as execute repairs
- ☐ Physical coordination—using multiple muscle movements to a single end, such as needed in athletics, skilled trades, etc.
- ☐ Organizing supplies or implements—able to identify methods that lead to ease of retrieval and maintenance
- ☐ Taking physical risks—attracted to activities or occupations with elements of physical danger
- ☐ Emotional stability, reliability—able to react impersonally to situations and thereby stay on course

Investigative Life Gifts

- ☐ Inventing—to imagine or produce something useful, especially in technical, scientific, or theoretical realms
- ☐ Researching—investigating or experimenting to get information, examine theories, or find new applications of current knowledge
- ☐ Conceptualizing—originating and developing abstract ideas or theories
- ☐ Working independently—able to work well without guidance or input from others
- ☐ Solving complex problems—able to find solutions to difficult situations or unique issues, usually through logic or knowledge base
- ☐ Computer aptitude—adept at systems and software design and development
- ☐ Synthesizing information—organizing or combining information from different sources so that it is easily understood
- ☐ Theorizing—articulating explanations, finding connections, or projecting future trends

Artistic Life Gifts

☐ Acting—projecting emotions or character by performing roles, either formally in theater settings or informally

☐ Writing, reporting, technical writing—able to communicate clearly through written words, including reports, letters, and publications

☐ Verbal/linguistics skills—adept at studying or learning languages, using and comprehending spoken words

☐ Musical expression—able to compose music or perform musically, either with voice, body, or instruments

☐ Creative problem-solving—able to find unusual solutions to issues, especially in artistic or interpersonal areas

☐ Sculpting/photography/graphic arts/painting—creative expression through artistic mediums

☐ Creative design through use of space—able to work with spatial concepts, as in interior design or architecture

☐ Creative expression through color—able to coordinate colors and patterns, as in clothing design, decorating, etc.

Social Life Gifts

☐ Teaching—instructing, demonstrating, training, or guiding the study of others so that they can learn facts or concepts

☐ Listening and facilitating—able to encourage others to volunteer information and discuss issues or topics, either one-on-one or in groups

☐ Understanding or counseling others—able to give appropriate advice and guidance tailored to the needs of others

☐ Conversing/informing—offering hospitality, talking and listening informally with one or a few others about daily events, issues, or personal concerns

☐ Being of service—considering and acting to aid the welfare of others

- [ ] Evaluating people's character—able to discern the motives and values of other people
- [ ] Being empathetic and tactful—aware of the feelings of others, able to adjust one's own behavior and respond accordingly
- [ ] Working with others—able to establish harmonious working relationships based on trust and synergy

Enterprising Life Gifts

- [ ] Public speaking—able to communicate clearly in front of a live audience
- [ ] Selling—able to convince others to purchase products or services
- [ ] Persuading—advocating the acceptance by others of ideas, values, or points of view
- [ ] Leadership—able to influence others to work together and direct people's efforts toward common missions goals
- [ ] Management—planning, organizing, and directing projects and resources to attain goals
- [ ] Negotiating—able to aid others in listening to diverse opinions or demands so as to reach agreement or compromise
- [ ] Taking action—responding decisively in emergency or stressful situations
- [ ] Adventurousness—able to take above-average financial and interpersonal risks

Conventional Life Gifts

- [ ] Organizing—able to arrange records, finances, offices, production lines, homes, etc., in a structured manner
- [ ] Appraising/evaluating—able to accurately estimate the value or significance of investments, antiques, real estate, business opportunities, etc.

- Attending to detail—aware of the small elements that make up the whole, as in printed words, administrative tasks, or the environment
- Managing time, setting priorities—arranging activities and schedules so that deadlines, appointments, and goals are consistently met
- Calculating and mathematical skills—adept at working with numbers and figures; adding, subtracting, multiplying, dividing
- Systematizing—classifying information or things for ease of use
- Persistence—exhibiting follow-through and patience when handling responsibilities
- Stewardship—conservative handling of money, data, things, and people

Spiritual Gifts

- Administration—the ability to organize information, events, or material to work efficiently for the body of Christ
- Apostleship—the ability to minister transculturally, starting new churches or ministries that impact multiple churches
- Discernment—the ability to recognize what is of God and what is not of God
- Encouragement/counseling—the ability to effectively listen to people, comforting and assisting them in moving toward psychological and relational wholeness
- Evangelism—the ability to spread the Good News of Jesus Christ to those who don't know him in a way that makes them respond in faith and discipleship
- Faith—the ability to recognize what God wants accomplished as well as to sustain a stalwart belief that God will see it done despite what others perceive as barriers
- Giving—the ability to give of material wealth freely and with joy to further God's causes

- ☐ Healing—the ability to call on God for the curing of illness and the restoration of health in a supernatural way
- ☐ Helps—the ability to work alongside others, attaching spiritual value to practical, often behind-the-scenes tasks that sustain the body of Christ
- ☐ Hospitality—the ability to provide a warm welcome for people that demonstrates God's love by providing food, shelter, or fellowship
- ☐ Knowledge—the ability to understand, organize, and effectively use information, either from natural sources or the Holy Spirit directly, for the advancement of God's purposes
- ☐ Leadership—the ability to motivate, coordinate, and direct the efforts of others in doing God's work
- ☐ Mercy—the ability to perceive the suffering of others and comfort and minister effectively with empathy
- ☐ Miracles—the ability to call on God to do supernatural acts that glorify him
- ☐ Prophecy—the ability to proclaim God's truths in a way relevant to current situations and to envision how God would will things to change
- ☐ Shepherding—the ability to guide and care for other Christians as they experience spiritual growth
- ☐ Teaching—the ability to understand and communicate God's truths to others effectively—in ways that lead to applications in their lives
- ☐ Tongues—the ability to speak in a language, known or unknown to others, supernaturally
- ☐ Interpretation of tongues—the ability to interpret spiritual languages
- ☐ Wisdom—the ability to understand and apply biblical and spiritual knowledge to complex, paradoxical, or other difficult situations

Appendix B

Suggestions for Small Group Discussion

Chapter 1. "If God Is My Copilot, Why Can't I Read the Instrument Panel?"

1. To acquaint everyone with the topic of looking for God's guidance, the small group leader can share some of his or her life decisions and let everyone second-guess how they were made. Examples might be a career decision, a major purchase, a move, etc.

2. The chapter lists several traps that keep people from seeking God's guidance. Which of these are traps for you?
   - A fear of flying—assuming that God's will for their life is a path to misery
   - Doubting the instrument readings—allowing uncertainty to paralyze us
   - Depending on signal lights—wanting tangible proof of God's will

- Expecting a smooth flight—assuming that troubles mean we've missed God's guidance

3. Read Psalm 143: 8, 10. What does a life on level ground look like? What can you expect?

4. Divide into two groups, or brainstorm each side of this question separately: what problems arise when you hold either of these positions?
- God always leads us directly and personally.
- God never leads us directly and personally.

5. Reread God's words to Moses (on page 15). Have you received certainty of God's guidance only *after* acting? Was this text a surprise to you?

6. We describe a life guided by God:

> And, as you go about living this worthy life, realize that you've already won the race—that's the freedom we have in Christ and it's what allowed Paul to put his past behind him. That's the attitude with which we can approach finding God's will—we have the freedom to do our best. It's an adventure where we're guaranteed a safe ending, knowing that even if we somehow misstep, God will help us back on course.

How does this agree with or differ from your vision of a guided life?

7. Encourage everyone to keep a journal of their "Reflections for Your Own LifeDirections" throughout your weeks together.

Chapter 2. What Has God Already Told Us? Finding Guidance Through Scripture

1. The small group leader can start the discussion by sharing a decision he or she made based on Scripture and allowing the group to second-guess his or her reasoning.

2. Have everyone bring in their favorite Bible study tools: concordances, study guides, computer software, etc. Share what you've found most helpful.

3. What most keeps you from Bible study?
   - Busyness?
   - Lack of good tools?
   - Difficulty finding others to study with?
   - It's boring?

   Brainstorm as a group how to get started (keeping in mind the different psychological types of the group members).

4. Read together Romans 14. What does Paul mean by disputable matters? Think of modern-day disagreements within the church. Which, according to this chapter, might be considered disputable matters? (Don't break into a dispute as you discuss this!)

5. Leaders at Jane and David's church often state, "We don't worship the Bible. We worship God." What is the difference and how might it help in using the Bible?

6. When you think about your weekly decisions, how, if at all, does the Bible influence your choices?

Chapter 3. How Has God Designed Us? Finding Guidance Through Our Special Design

1. The small group leader can start the discussion by sharing a decision he or she made based on his or her special design and allowing the group to second-guess the reasoning.

2. Look through the main points of the chapter (page 88ff.) and discuss whether any of them were new to you.

3. What parts of your special design are you aware of currently? Has this knowledge influenced your life choices?

4. Read together Steve's story on page 65. What is your view on Christian service?

5. Share how much of your time you get to use your gifts. If it is less than 60 percent, is this temporary or chronic? Discuss as a group how God might lead you through your giftedness in this way.

Chapter 4. Listening to the Holy Spirit: Does God Ever Speak Directly?

1. The small group leader can give an example of direct guidance through the Spirit and ask for other experiences.

2. Review the main points of the chapter on page 120ff. Discuss any main insights group members gained from this chapter.

3. What is your overall reaction to this chapter?

4. Take a group survey. Who has experienced direct leadings through dreams? Prophecies? Images or vision? Angels? Direct commands? Let everyone who wants to share an experience, and also whether or not they always considered it a direct leading.

5. Set ground rules for this question. Let people state which form of direct guidance is hardest for them to believe in, then let someone share a story about experiencing this form of guidance and why they're certain it was from God. Then without any further discussion, go on to the next person to hear their difficulty with this topic.

Chapter 5. What Is Happening in the World Around Me? Being Guided by Circumstances

1. The small group leader can begin discussion by sharing a situation for the group to work through using the steps on pages 157ff.

2. Look through the main points of the chapter on page 160. Discuss the main insights you received through this chapter.

3. The chapter points out that God's guidance is usually a lamp unto our feet, not a lighthouse beaming into the future. How far would you really like that light to shine into the future?

4. Discuss techniques for using your values to evaluate your circumstances.

5. Share times where you learned a lesson through circumstances that you didn't know you needed.

6. Ask one of the group members to share a circumstantial situation he or she or someone they know has faced. Then work through what you learned in this chapter to discuss what God might be doing.

Chapter 6. All Systems Go! Integrating the Four Guidance Systems

1. If the small group leader has a mission statement, share with the group a specific time it helped you in making a decision.

2. Look through the main points of the chapter on pages 184–185 and discuss any major insights you had.

3. "If you hold to my teaching, you are really my disciples. Then you will know the truth, and the truth will set you free" (John 8:32). How have you found this to be true?

4. Share which life gifts and which spiritual gifts help you in decision-making (refer to Appendix A). Help one another discover how else you might use your gifts to look for God's guidance.

5. Choose any one of the following texts from the book of Acts and see if as a group you can find how each of the four guidance systems was used:
   • Philip and the Eunuch (Acts 8:26-39)
   • Peter and Cornelius (Acts 10)
   • Paul and Timothy, for Athens
   • Ananias and Paul (Acts 9:1-19)

6. On page 174, there is a list of promises Michelle recalled as she looked for God's guidance. As a group, share Bible references that have helped you. Use the endpages of this book to record the verse references. Later, you can look them up and write in the texts or add more of your own.

7. "I think we gain the power to do God's will as we step forward in faith, even if we can't survey the final destination." When have you been encouraged to follow leaders who have stepped out in faith? How does this apply to your life?

Chapter 7. Flying in Formation: Finding Guidance in Community

1. Share any experiences you've had in making decisions with the goal being the kind of unity this chapter describes.

2. Look back through the chapter's main points on page 200 and discuss any major insights.

3. Do you view this model of decision-making as realistic? Utopian? Impractical? Read together Chuck Colson's quote on pages 197–198. Can you refute it?

4. What do you think blocks the church from this type of decision-making?

5. "Think about this: The Christian church isn't a democracy. God is at the head, making all the decisions. We're supposed to work together as the unified body of Christ to follow God's instructions." Does this make sense? Why or why not?

6. Which usually fails first for you? Endurance to continue the process until you reach unity or your ability to encourage others to persevere?

7. Reread the ground rules for making decisions as a group. Which are the hardest for you to carry out?

Chapter 8. All in God's Good Timing: A Few Final Guiding Thoughts

1. As you think about stepping out to allow God to guide you, what questions or concerns do you still have?

2. Covenant as a group to trace a major decision in one another's lives, using the four guidance systems, over the next three months. Review where you are each week and report in on what God has done.

3. Read together Hebrews 12:1. What hinders you as you try to listen for God's four guidance systems?

4. "Wherever you are standing—close to God or far away, in trust or in doubt, in confusion or with confidence—someone else has been there before you, asking the same questions of God and wondering where to turn." How does this "cloud of witnesses" encourage you as you try to understand God's will for your life?

Appendix C

Integrating God's Guidance for Your Life Decisions

Make as many copies of the following pages as you wish to guide you through decisions you may face. For some choices, the suggested level of detail will be too great; for others, the questions may help to remind you of the many ways in which God might be guiding you.

Consider keeping a copy of this tool in your daily planner, journal, or purse, so that you always have a place to record insights.

Experiencing God's Guidance Through Scripture

For this situation, for this decision, or for today, the Bible, augmented by other Christian wisdom, seems to be providing me with guidance in the following ways:

General Insights: Is this matter disputable or nondisputable? What moral principles or ideas seem to apply?

Verse or passage reference   Relevant message for me right now

Bible stories or characters: Is my situation similar to any stories of the Bible? What can I learn from the examples of the people in the Bible?

Specific leadings as I read and study Scripture: In my regular study, have any verses "spoken" to me, or have certain verses come to mind that seem to have special meaning in my situation?

Verse or passage reference   Relevant message for me right now

Do others agree with my interpretation? Remember, God's guidance is a light for our journey, not a full map.

Experiencing God's Guidance Through Your Special Design

For this situation, for this decision, or for today, my special, God-given design (gifts, personality, values, passions) seems to be providing me with guidance in the following ways:

Life Gifts and Spiritual Gifts

Alternative choices I have	Gifts I believe are needed for each choice	Do I have this gift?	What is God saying about my choices through how I am gifted?

Psychological Type: As I review the places or atmospheres that best fit my type, what guidance might God be providing about my choices?

How might my psychological type help/hinder this decision? (see pages 82–83).

Passions and Interests: Ignoring the "practical" considerations for a moment, what are my passions or interests right now? Are they changing? Is God trying to lead me toward something new I might do *en theos*, enthusiastically with God?

Values: What values, beliefs, principles, etc., are core to me in this situation? Which can't be overlooked? Am I paying attention to the values God wants me to hold today for this decision?

Experiencing God's Guidance Through the Spirit

For this situation, for this decision, or for today, God seems to be providing me with direct guidance through the Holy Spirit in the following ways:

Direct Leadings: Have I paid attention to the variety of ways in which God may be trying to get my attention? What messages might God be giving me through these avenues?
- dreams
- the words or prophecies of other people
- images or visions
- angels
- direct commands

Ideally, how would I like God to direct me for this situation? What further guidance do I need in order to know for certain the choices to make?

Am I erring by either waiting for the certainty the Spirit could provide, ignoring the other guidance systems, or assuming the Spirit won't provide further guidance?

Have I prayed and asked for guidance and wisdom for this decision? What, if any, inputs have come as a result?

Experiencing God's Guidance Through Circumstances

For this situation, for this decision, or for today, God seems to be providing me with direct guidance through my circumstances in the following ways:

The Evidence

The facts of my situation	Does this indicate an open door? How?	Does this indicate a closed door? How?

The Interpretation: As I pray about this situation, are the facts the only message? What is God trying to say to me through them?

Am I dismissing anything as a simple coincidence that may be a bigger message from God?

As I share this story with others, what other interpretations do they make?

Are all of these choices within God's will? Is God telling me that any choice is fine?

The Standard: Am I making any decisions or taking as guidance anything that contradicts the wisdom and timeless standards of the Bible?

Summary

Use this page to restate the insights you received from:

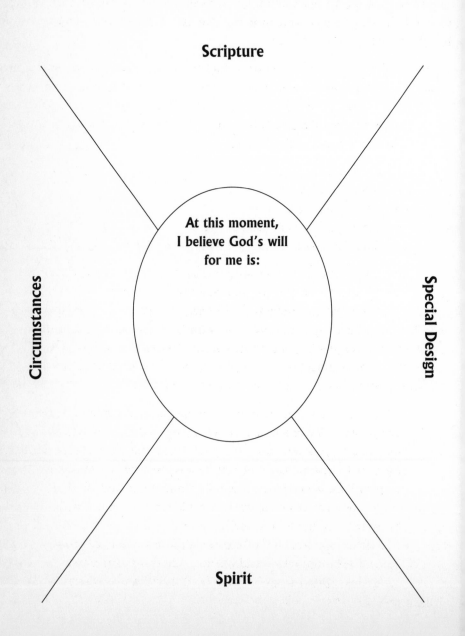

Scripture

Circumstances

Special Design

At this moment,
I believe God's will
for me is:

Spirit